THE
EIGHT-FINGERED
CRIMINAL'S SON

For Eric —

William Snyder

THE
EIGHT-FINGERED
CRIMINAL'S SON

A COLLECTION OF MOSTLY
TRUE STORIES

WILLIAM SNYDER

CACTUS SURF PRESS
2011

ISBN -13:978-1468142587
ISBN -10:1468142585

First Printing

A note on the cover: The man in the photograph, circa 1960, is none other than William "Cash" Snyder.

This book is presented as a work of fiction and any similitude between the characters and persons living or dead is merely coincidental and all that jazz.

I wish to express my gratitude to Clifton Batchelor, Robert Sanchez, Bryan Frank, John Marcilionis, and Tony Frink for their invaluable encouragement, assistance and support.

for the eight-fingered criminal's wife

TABLE OF CONTENTS

Author's Note : My grandfather used to say, "Never let the truth get in the way of a good story." Hold on, that's not true at all. It was the truck driver who lived across the street that used to throw the expression around. But doesn't it sound a heckuva of a lot better coming from my grandfather?

THE
EIGHT-FINGERED
CRIMINAL'S SON

THE
EIGHT-FINGERED
CRIMINAL'S SON

1960

I was born and raised in Hawthorne, a working class suburb of Los Angeles, California. When it comes to my formative years, my father was generally out of the picture. As of this writing, I don't know whether he is alive or dead. I do know that he was once tall and lean and charismatic. I know that he went by the name of Cash and his forearms were covered with tattoos. And I know that he robbed liquor stores and spent a few years in prison. When I was very young, he returned in the middle of the night, perhaps from jail. The dark room exploded with stinging white light as the unfamiliar man snatched me up close to his cheek, sharp whiskers jabbing against my face. The smell of whiskey, cigarettes and aftershave overpowered me as he kissed me on the forehead.

"Billy, do you want to come live with me?"

The last place I wanted to be was anywhere this strange man might be going. Tears rolled down his cheeks as I shook my head no.

Another of my father's brief homecomings took place a few years later when he rolled up in front of the apartment building behind the wheel of a shiny new powder blue convertible.

"Where'd you get that?" I asked.

Triumphantly, he flashed the palm of his right hand. I was shocked at the sight of two grisly stubs where his index and middle fingers had once been.

"Not a bad deal for a couple a measly fingers, huh, Billy boy?"

When I asked him if he'd really paid for the car with his fingers, he told me that in a way he had. Years later my mother explained that he had lost the fingers in a machine shop accident, that he received insurance money to buy the car. One of my uncles insisted the finger story was more complicated, more disreputable than a simple machine shop accident. At any rate, Cash took the family on elaborate celebratory outings to Disneyland, Knott's Berry Farm, and Griffith Park. And then he was gone, not to be seen again for another five years.

LEE HARVEY OSWALD

1963

It was 1963. My grandmother and I were in a Sears department store elevator. The doors glided silently open. An enormous black woman filled the doorway. Her face was soaked with tears. "They killed Kennedy!" she shrieked between sobs. I looked up to my grandmother and she was crying too. Scanning the towering occupants of the elevator, they were all bawling and things seemed out of control. The world had evidently been turned upside down and I was scared to death.

My memory jump cuts to the dinner table at my grandparents' home. A painting of John F. Kennedy and another of the blonde, blue-eyed surfer version of Jesus Christ hung on the wall behind my grandfather. We were eating Jell-O with tiny chunks of pears, peaches and bananas bouncing around inside. My grandfather, who had been eating in silence, suddenly slammed his great lumberman's fist on the table, shouting, "God dammit! I knew they'd never let a Catholic run this country!" My Jell-O reverberated wildly in the glass bowl.

My memory jump cuts again. This time the picture is crystal clear. I sit with my legs crossed, Indian style, on the colossal oval rug in front of my grandparents' black and white television set. Carefully, I watch the scene for what must be the fifteenth time. Lee Harvey Oswald's hands are cuffed as he rounds the corner in the underground parking structure. Dwarfed by giant grey men in cowboy hats, he wears a five o'clock shadow and looks an awful lot like one of the guys who works on cars behind my apartment building. I hate him because he is the man who killed the Catholic president. The fedora wearing Chicago gangster appears from nowhere, his back to the camera. I know that his name is Jack Ruby. The gangster bum-rushes Oswald as the towering cowboy policemen stand by – useless. There is the muffled sound of gunshots. Oswald's face appears almost comical. His eyes are shut and he looks as though he is trying very hard to whistle.

This unbelievably violent, chaotic, enigmatic scene is cemented into the foundations of the husband, father, and teacher I have since become.

MY GRANDPARENTS' HOUSE

1966

The real action of my early years took place at my grandparents' house on 142nd Street. It was a magical place. By grownup standards, the lot extended back no further than a regulation sized basketball court, some ninety-four feet or so. But from my own child's eyes, the place was some kind of sprawling adventure land. Two enormous palm trees stood on either side of the front lawn which was split down the middle by a cracking white cement walkway.

A covered porch jutted out from the front of the house to meet the walkway. My grandmother's prized hydrangea bushes sat on either side of the porch. Consisting of thousands of tiny purple flowers, the gorgeous purple blooms were about the size and shape of a half-cantaloupe, round side up. The scent morphed from sweet to oppressive when the sun went down. The porch itself was elevated high enough that a fall could cause serious injury. I know this because I was a party to, if not the cause of one such injury. My mother was standing on the porch holding my sister Linda in her arms. Linda was three and I was six and I don't exactly remember who started the ruckus. It could be that my sister kicked me in the head. Perhaps I gave the loose skin of her arm a good hard pinch. The bottom line is we went at it, her kicking with her free leg and me socking away with Kato like fists of fury, causing my mother to lose her balance and plunge into the hydrangea bushes below.

"Oh my God! My leg! My leg!" my mother screamed.

She was rolling around in the bushes, writhing in agony.

My grandfather kept saying, "Get up Helen! Walk it off!"

My mother did not walk it off. Instead, she spent the next couple of months with her right leg in a white plaster cast.

KOOKIE THE WONDER DOG

1964

Two narrow strips of splintering, ashen concrete crept along the side of the house. Green and yellow weeds sprouted from cracks. Leading up to a battered wooden garage, the driveway was bisected by a rickety swinging gate that separated the front and back yards. It was at this gate that my faithful pooch Kookie the Wonder Dog nearly met an early demise.

I was just a squirt, five years old, six at best. My Uncle Ronnie, who was attending UCLA, was hanging out in the back yard with some of his cronies. All of them sported crew cuts. They stood around smoking Kools and drinking cans of Schlitz beer. Each of them was dressed in cuffed Levis and an unbuttoned Pendleton worn over a pressed white t-shirt.

One of the guys was tossing sticks for Kookie the Wonder Dog. Kookie was a victim of OCDFD, otherwise known as

Obsessive Compulsive Doggy Fetching Disorder. The amazing mutt had a true need to fetch. And she would fetch anything; sticks, rocks, bricks, it didn't matter. I can remember throwing the same rock for her into a river for several hours. I guess I was easily entertained at the time. Kookie kept diving, sometimes twenty or thirty times on one rock fetching trip, but she never failed to come back with the same rock that I had thrown.

Half dachshund and half beagle, that was the heritage some veterinarian had determined for her. The loveable dog had followed my father home from a bar one Friday night. I was told she was named after the subject of the song with the line: *Kookie, Kookie, lend me your comb.* The poor mutt was covered with fleas, sometimes freeways of fleas commuted from one end of her body to the other. I can remember spending hours hunting the fleas through the short brown fur on Kookie's back. Fastidiously, I ran my fingers through her fur until I spotted one of the little devils. Then I would pinch it in half between my fingernails. I was a respectable flea hunter. Her floppy ears were ripped and shredded like the frills of a buckskin shirt. This was due to Kookie's unfriendly relationship with the German Shepherd down the street at the Flourchamp's place. The two dogs fought viciously and often. She survived being run over by cars time after time. And somehow that flea-ridden mutt lived to be more than twenty years of age.

Just for the heck of it, one of my uncle's buddies picked up a two-by-four and heaved it over the gate and into the front yard. Kookie was on that two-by-four like a cheap suit. Balancing the piece of wood between her choppers, she headed for the back yard at full speed. There was a problem. The gate was a couple of feet narrower than the two-by-four. Physics took over when that hunk of wood slammed into the immovable objects that were the gateposts. That little dog was propelled a full fifteen feet into the weathered wooden garage door. SMACK. For a split second, Kookie the Wonder Dog stuck to that garage door like a bug to a windshield. Then she slid to the cement driveway where she lay with her legs saluting the sun like a dead cockroach.

"You killed my sister's dog, you dumb son of a bitch!" my uncle sneered, grabbing hold of the guy's Pendleton and shoving him into the aluminum trashcans, spilling corn rinds, coffee grounds, cigarette butts and beer cans all over the driveway. The two were trading brutal punches to the face and wrestling in the garbage when Kookie came to, gave her head a good shake and waddled to the front yard. She dragged the two-by-four into the back yard and began barking for someone to play fetch with her. The combatants stopped pummeling each other and looked at the mutt as if she were some kind of doggy ghost.

Kookie truly was the Wonder Dog.

A TWO-BY-FOUR WITH A WHOLE MESS OF NAILS

1965

The most mysterious place within the confines of my grandparents' property was inside the garage where it was dark and smelled of sawdust, rotting wood, paint thinner and gasoline. Heaps of sawdust blanketed the cement floor. An endless supply of two-by-fours, sawhorses, rakes and shovels, some broken and some not, saws, screwdrivers, and hammers could be found in the recesses of that garage. A kid had to keep his good stuff close when wandering through that garage. The strange old building had a tendency to swallow up prized possessions like magnifying glasses and slingshots and PF Flyer secret decoder rings. There were nails too, every kind of nail that could be imagined. There were thousands, maybe millions of nails in that old weather beaten garage. The nails were stored in pickle jars, jelly jars, peanut butter jars and just about any other jar known to mankind and they were scattered throughout the garage. A never ending array of jars stuffed with nails could be seen on shelves lining the walls, on the workbenches and under the workbenches. Those jars of nails were everywhere. There were snowshoes, tennis shoes, football cleats, golf shoes, surfboards, fishing nets, suitcases, ancient trunks, misshapen birdcages, and aquariums with cracked glass. And there were pick axes, croquet mallets, rotting tennis rackets, disassembled M-16s and beaver traps. That's right; I said there were disassembled M-16s and beaver traps. One of my uncles figured out a way to bring the broken M-16s back from Vietnam and my grandfather had once trapped beaver for extra cash. Life sized wooden cutouts of the Baby Jesus, Mary and Joseph, shepherds, wise men, Santa Claus and the reindeer could all be seen peering down from the rafters, waiting for my grandfather to set them up in his elaborate front yard Christmas display. Michelangelo's Sistine Chapel ceiling had nothing on the great collective work of art that was the awe inspiring masterpiece in the rafters of my grandparents' garage.

My early memories involve rummaging through that garage with my cousins Roxanne and Dusty, who were a bit older than me, and Ronnie, who was a bit younger. We practiced hammering for hours on end, pounding hundreds, maybe thousands of nails into the eternal supply of my grandfather's soft white pine two-by-fours. And then we would drag these deadly two-by-fours out into the back yard and heave them at the trees, experiencing great amazement when the hunks of wood actually stuck to the trunks.

The backyard was filled with wonder and mystery. Exotic sounds could be heard from the other side of the rickety wooden fence. The next door neighbors kept a pet chimpanzee by the name of Dwight David Eisenhower.

Late one Friday night my uncle had come home and was trying to get a little shut-eye in the bedroom that had been built onto the back of the garage. The chimp was in heat and she was making a terrible racket. Yes, it's true; Dwight David Eisenhower was a girl. Uncle Ronnie yelled at the beast, ordering it to pipe down but the thing only got louder. Boiling with rage, my uncle stormed outside and heaved a beer bottle, sending it crashing loudly onto the aluminum roof of the chimp's cage. The chimp noise stopped. Satisfied, my uncle turned to head back to bed and was promptly nailed in the back of the noggin with the bottle. The chimp had returned fire. Dwight David Eisenhower may have been a girl but she certainly did not throw like one.

In that magnificent back yard there were more hydrangeas and rose bushes with razor sharp thorns. A vast abandoned birdhouse, containing three separate rooms, sat in the middle of the lawn. It was covered with chicken wire and the floor consisted of sand and decade old canary droppings. Next to the colossal birdcage was a derelict convertible with a shattered windshield. The glass covered the front seat and floor boards. Someone was always getting sliced up on the glass.

This was another time, a time before tetanus shots and bicycle helmets. Kids were allowed to be kids and fall down and scrape their knees and bang their heads on the concrete. It was a time when kids didn't wear shoes. I can recall stubbing my big toe – a lot. It's a vivid childhood memory, stubbing my big toe. I can clearly remember tearing down the sidewalk at full speed. And then, for some ungodly, unknown reason, one of my big toes catches on the sidewalk or the asphalt. My toe stops, but the rest of my foot keeps pushing forward, pushing my fat little big toe under and ripping the skin. And there I am left with a large flap of skin hanging loose from the front of my bloody, fat, little big toe.

I have since talked to other adults about the commonality of the flapping hunk of skin over my big toe in my early years. And you know, no one else seems to have been able to recount similar memories. People have suggested that, perhaps, I was the unfortunate victim of a developmentally retarded running style.

There were wandering desert tortoises in that backyard, lots of them, and there was Cyclops the one eyed cat. My cousins and I spent untold hours attempting to corner and get our mitts on that scraggly orange cat. We all were, at one time or another, the victims of his vicious, razor sharp claw defenses. Every once in a while, somebody would catch that mean, old, scraggly, orange cat and pin down all four legs just so we could stare into the gaping pink chasm that had once been filled with Cyclops's left eye ball.

The backyard grass and weeds grew shoulder high to a child. My grandfather only mowed a couple of times a year. In his defense, it was a nightmare of a job when the grass was three feet high.

I can remember sprinting barefoot through the grass, chasing Cyclops the one eyed cat and suddenly experiencing a bizarre sensation smack dab in the middle of the bottom of my right foot. It wasn't until I tried to raise my foot that I felt the weight of the two-by-four followed by the white-hot pain caused by the rusty nail that had plunged at least an inch into my arch.

"ARGHH!"

I collapsed. My cousins encircled me, oblivious to the giant hunk of wood that was nailed to my foot beneath the jungle grass.

"What's a matter Billy?" Dusty asked.

"ARGH! MY FOOT! I STEPPED ON A NAIL! ARGH!"

They knelt and cleared the grass to investigate.

"ARGHHH!" I screamed some more.

"AHHH!" they all joined me in screaming when they got a look at the bloody horrible two-by-four and the rusty nail and foot that were all one piece. This was much more gruesome than Cyclops' pink scabbed-over eye socket.

"Let me get it out," Dusty said, making a move toward the wood.

"NO! DON'T TOUCH IT!" I screamed.

I was up on my good foot in a split second, hysterically flopping around the back yard. Each time I attempted to lift the impaled foot, I experienced weird, unbearable pain. I could feel that rusty nail pressing against the bone in my foot. Oh, the horror. I was out of my mind, screaming bloody impalement. The hysteria broke when my grandmother arrived on the scene to slam me, face first, to the ground, sit on my back, facing my feet and rip the two-by-four loose from my foot. I don't remember much after that. I was probably delirious and in some form of shock. I'm sure she carried me into the bathroom, stuck my foot in a tub of hot water and then cleaned the gaping wound out with Q-tips dipped in alcohol and Mercurochrome. Like I said, there were no trips to the emergency room for tetanus shots in those days.

My early childhood was strange and hectic and even frightening at times.

I'll tell you one thing – now that I am an adult, I do make it a point never to allow my children to hammer a bunch of nails into two-by-fours and leave them out on the back lawn and let the grass grow six months and then allow those kids to run around the backyard without any shoes on their feet.

Not me.

Never.

Some lessons are learned early in life.

DANNY GILROY'S PENCIL

1968

The life of a fourth grader at Saint Joseph's Parish School was no walk in the park. To begin with, we had to deal with Sister Agnes. She was the scariest nun I had ever known. Unless she's a hundred and sixty years old, the woman is dead by now. And I guess its bad form to disrespect the deceased. To tell you the truth, Sister Agnes looked like a corpse even when she was alive. The old gal was unbelievably emaciated, looking very much like a plucked chicken. Her pallid, cracked skin was pulled tight against her face while scraggly bright red hairs shot out from under her black and white penguin habit. Her dental situation was a real mess; about twice the size of normal teeth, yellow choppers jutted out from her gums in every direction but up and down. I tried to follow her instructions because her lips rose up when she screamed at us, exposing those horrible, yellow teeth. Like all of the nuns, Sister Agnes was more than willing to whack me upside the head with the flat of her hand or pummel my knuckles with the hard side of a ruler. She was a terrible teacher. The woman raced through math concepts and refused to field questions. Math class for me was constant bewilderment. My mother had to hire a tutor so I could pass the fourth grade.

Sister Agnes told us creepy stories we knew to be hogwash, but they held our attention nonetheless. Once, she went into a tirade about the dangers of throwing snowballs. In the twenty-nine years I lived in Hawthorne, California, it never snowed. Not once. Yet Sister Agnes felt compelled to deliver her cautionary tale.

When I was in the fifth grade, I lived in Boston. Even though we had been warned that it was dangerous to throw snowballs, some of the children failed to heed the advice of caring adults. I remember one particular day, school had let out and I was on my way home. A disobedient boy by the name of Jimmy Dolan began throwing snowballs at some of the children. One of the boys took careful aim and heaved an icy snowball back at Jimmy. Now boys and girls, that icy snowball hit Jimmy Dolan in the corner of his left eye and knocked his eyeball right out of the socket. And Jimmy ran home with his eyeball hanging from his eye socket by a string of tissue. The doctors couldn't save that eye and Jimmy Dolan wears a black eye patch to this day. So boys and girls, the next time one of you thinks you want to throw a snowball at somebody, just take a moment to remember poor Jimmy Dolan and his black eye patch.

Although I'm sure the story never happened, I do think of Jimmy Dolan's black eye patch and get the heebie-jeebies when I see a movie in which someone heaves a snowball. That nun really got deep into my psyche. I guess that's what nuns do. I clearly remember wondering what it would be like to have my eyeball swinging from the socket by a two-foot string. Would I still be able to see from the swinging eyeball? If I held the eyeball behind my head, could I see what was going on behind me?

I attended my Cub Scout den meeting every Wednesday after school. The story of Danny Gilroy's pencil actually begins at one such den meeting. Mrs. Allen, the den mother, told us to pipe down so she could start the meeting. I was minding my own business, washing down a Chips Ahoy cookie with a big swig of milk, when Donald Allen executed this amazingly funny trick in which he made it appear that he was shoving his entire finger up his nostril. Thinking back, perhaps he did shove that finger all the way up his nostril. Either way, I must have thought it was pretty funny because I laughed so hard that my milk shot up my nose and out through my own nostrils. Somehow, in all the excitement, a chunk of cookie lodged itself in my throat. I must have turned blue fast because Mrs. Allen immediately wrapped her arms around me and lifted me from my chair, perfectly executing the Heimlich maneuver, catapulting that chunk of cookie across the kitchen, and sending it sliding across the shiny pink linoleum floor.

"What happened, Billy?" Mrs. Allen asked.

"Donald stuck his finger up his nose and it made me laugh."

Donald began to snicker. His mother leaned across the table with supernatural mom reach and smacked him hard on the back of the head.

"It's not funny, you idiot! This kid almost choked to death. You are in big trouble, mister."

Donald glared at me and I knew I would have to have to deal with him later. Donald Allen was a fifth grader and I didn't want any part of him. He was tougher than I was. Of course, that's not saying much. Donald's little sister was probably tougher than I was.

I managed to avoid Donald at school the next day. I avoided him, that is, until I made my way into the parking lot where my ride home Marge Hammervolt was waiting for me. Donald Allen was standing between me and Mrs. Hammervolt's faded 1935 yellow Woody.

"You finked on me, Snyder."

"I didn't mean to, Donald."

"Let's go, you and me, right now."

Donald held up his fists in a fighting stance.

"I would, but Mrs. Hammervolt's waiting and she's got to drive a lot of kids home."

"I'll fight him for you, Snyder," a voice interrupted from behind.

It was none other than David Lopez, the toughest kid in fourth grade. David Lopez was stocky, with a dark complexion, black hair hanging over his eyes and beads of sweat rolling down his face. David Lopez always had beads of sweat rolling down his face. In a meat locker, he would have had beads of sweat rolling down his face. Every kid in the fourth grade was scared to death of this kid. David Lopez wore pointy black boots for the sole purpose of inflicting great pain when he kicked some unlucky sucker in the nuts. He was always throwing his head back and laughing loud from the gut. I guess he was a kind of kid version of Ernest Borgnine. Allen was a little surprised by the challenge, but he shrugged okay. The two circled each other for about ten seconds. Then David Lopez gripped Donald's wrists, pulled the boy off balance and began spinning him the way a dad would with spin his kid in the park. Lopez spun my would-be ass whooper around at least ten times before letting go, sending him skidding across the asphalt parking lot. Lopez threw his head back and laughed from the gut. Donald Allen got up slowly and walked away. Black asphalt was ground into his elbows and the palms of his hands.

"Thanks for letting me fight him, Snyder," David Lopez said, genuinely grateful, before he turned and lumbered through the crowd of kids that had gathered for the showdown.

Mrs. Hammervolt honked the Woody horn, leaned out of the driver's side window and shouted, "Let's go, Billy." I guess it was my lucky day. Donald Allen never bothered me again.

Francis Rodriguez was the second toughest kid in the fourth grade. One day he was throwing the football with Jackie Greggor. Francis liked to zip the ball over Jackie's head so it would bean some poor unsuspecting sucker, usually in the head. I can tell you from experience that getting nailed in the skull by a football thrown by Francis Rodriguez was no joke. Francis Rodriguez was a superior athlete and he possessed a cannon for an arm. He would go on to play football for the USC Trojans. I can remember actually seeing stars and experiencing ringing between the ears after falling victim to a particularly painful Francis Rodriguez beaning. On this particular day, the second toughest kid in fourth grade made the tactical error of beaning the toughest kid in fourth grade right in the back of the melon.

Lopez staggered and wheeled around, madness in his eyes. The entire playground stopped. There was complete silence. It was just like the scene in the western movies when the saloon piano player stops playing. David Lopez was really hot, looking like one of those cartoon characters with the steam whistle blowing overhead. He trudged across the playground to where Francis was trying to look innocent. A mass of kids wearing white shirts and salt and pepper corduroys formed a giant circle around Lopez and Rodriguez.

"I guess you want to die, Francis."

Lopez's eyes looked crazy. It was the first time any of us had seen Francis Rodriguez show genuine fear like an actual human kid.

"Lopez, it was an accident."

Rodriguez was looking down at Lopez's nut kickers.

"Let's go, Francis," Lopez said, gesturing for Francis to step forward.

Sweat pouring from his forehead, Lopez began to circle Francis Rodriguez. The second toughest kid in the fourth grade reluctantly took his fighting stance. All of a sudden, Danny Gilroy broke through the crowd. Fast as lightning, he was behind David Lopez and he stabbed him square in the middle of the back with a brand new, freshly sharpened number two pencil. Gilroy didn't stop as he bolted past Lopez and Rodriguez and through the crowd. Lopez stood there frozen with the pencil sticking out from his back. The entire playground released a collective gasp. The pencil looked so strange and yellow protruding from the back of David Lopez's white uniform shirt.

Danny Gilroy was a wacky little kid with greased back hair, thick-framed glasses and an ever-present ear-to-ear grin on his face. He was one of those kids who could flip his eyelids inside out. His huge glasses magnified the pink insides of his eyelids, making the sight a class-A gross out. The kid wasn't afraid of Sister Agnes and the other nuns like the rest of us. He didn't seem to mind having his knuckles whacked by a ruler or getting nun-smacked in the head. He just looked at Sister Agnes or whoever was dishing out the corporal punishment and grinned his gigantic, ear-to-ear grin. Gilroy lived in his own world, man.

"What happened?" Lopez asked.

"Gilroy stabbed you in the back with a pencil, man," Tony Frink shouted from somewhere in the back of the crowd.

David Lopez roared like a wounded grizzly. His eyes became orbs of flaming red fire. Although Gilroy had a decent head start, Lopez took after him and gained on him fast. The toughest kid in the fourth grade had excellent foot speed for a big kid with a pencil sticking out of his back, but Gilroy was as fast as greased lightning. I wondered if Lopez was going to die. I thought back to an episode of *The Outer Limits* in which a man had died after being stabbed in the back by a burglar. Lopez chased Gilroy around the parking lot, through the church, and into the heavy traffic of Hawthorne Boulevard. Cars slammed on their breaks.

"Get out of the street, you stupid kids!" someone yelled from a faded yellow Plymouth Valiant.

When Sister Eugene Francesca rang her hand-held bell, signaling the end of lunch recess, David Lopez was still chasing that crazy kid. Lopez's back was soaked with sweat. There was no visible blood, just the pencil sticking out, bobbing up and down as he ran. It looked incredibly strange, almost hypnotic. The rest of the school had lined up for class and Lopez was still chasing the crazy little kid. Gilroy zipped by, just before Sister Mary Elizabeth, a nun of substantial girth, threw out her right arm and clothes-lined Lopez as he attempted to run by. Lopez did a complete flip and landed hard, face down in the asphalt. Gilroy kept running and he kept on grinning. Several nuns, volunteer mothers, the PE teacher and Monsignor Redehan, who was chomping on a jumbo sized cigar, were all chasing Danny Gilroy. It was crazy. Gilroy was dodging and juking, making the grown ups look utterly ridiculous. They chased Gilroy into the school compound. One of the nuns came out and asked Sister Mary Elizabeth to bring Lopez to the nurse's office. They walked away from us, Sister Mary Elizabeth's hand tightly gripped around the back of the David Lopez's neck and that yellow pencil wagging from the middle of his sweat soaked back like some kind of grotesque, mis-placed tail. Soon Sister Agnes came out to usher us back to class.

"Where's David Lopez?" Tony Frink asked.

"He's gone to the doctor for a tetanus shot," Sister Agnes replied.

"Is he going to die?" asked Margie Galindo.

"One never knows about these things. We can only pray that he has been to confession and asked forgiveness for his sins – in case he does die," Sister Agnes explained.

"Where is Danny Gilroy?" someone asked.

"Danny has gone to confession to ask the Lord's forgiveness."

I wondered why they didn't take Lopez to confession – in case he died. David Lopez did not die. He was back at school the next day. He never did beat the snot out of Francis Rodriguez. In fact, it wasn't long before the two of them were laughing and beaning kids with the football together. Danny Gilroy did not come back to school – ever. Nobody saw or heard from Danny Gilroy again. There was a rumor that Gilroy had been committed to a mental hospital, and another that he was sent to a maximum security prison for kids in Utah. No one knows why Danny Gilroy chose to act as Francis Rodriguez's personal guardian angel that day. Did he hate David Lopez that much? Or was it that he liked Rodriguez that much? Perhaps it was just a whim. We had all seen Danny Gilroy do a lot of things that didn't make sense. If nothing else, Sister Agnes had the makings of a new cautionary tale to go with her snowball story.

DUAL DREAMS AND JOHN HALE

1968-1976
Dreams are wiser than men.
-Omaha Saying

1.

I found myself shuffling through the playground sand at Hawthorne Memorial Park on the corner of Prairie and El Segundo. It was 1968 and I was in the fourth grade. The park was absolutely deserted. The silence was complete. There were no cars on the road, no other kids, no old Italians playing bocce ball, no planes in the sky. I was feeling kind of lonely when I noticed John Hale from Saint Joseph's swinging on the monkey bars. He was wearing his signature thick black-rimmed glasses and our school uniform, a neatly pressed white collared shirt and salt and pepper corduroy pants.

"Hale!" I shouted.

The kid was doing some amazing things on those monkey bars. He looked like some kind of gymnast, expertly swinging up and over the bars. John Hale was a pretty good athlete, one of the best in the fourth grade, but these moves were darned near impossible.

"Hale!" I shouted again as I sprinted toward the monkey bars.

"Hi, Snyder."

"What are you doing here?"

John Hale let go of the bar, tucked and perfectly executed three flips. In the same motion, impossible as it seemed, he blasted upward to the square platform at the top of the winding, metal slide. Dumbfounded, I executed a *Little Rascals* style double take. Something wasn't right.

"What the heck? How did you do that, Hale?"

"We're in a dream, Snyder," Hale said matter-of-factly. "You can do anything you want in a dream."

"Are you kidding me?"

"Do I look like I'm kidding, Snyder?"

He grinned widely as he hopped down from the platform, walked over to the basketball court and casually picked up a weathered red, white and blue ABA style ball that just happened to be sitting at mid-court. John Hale began to dribble the ball. Picking up speed, he showed a few moves that would have put Walter Clyde Frazier himself to shame. Upon reaching the free throw line, he leapt into the sky, soared toward the basket and threw down a crushing, rim-rattling, two-handed Wilt Chamberlain style dunk.

"Whoa!"

"Go ahead. Why don't you try something, Snyder? You do realize that nothing's impossible in a dream, don't you?"

Taking a couple of steps, I leapt into the sky. I was flying. That's all there was to it. Absolutely weightless, I shot rapidly above the park and into the clouds. The cool pristine breeze rushed against my face. Freedom. Hale was right. I really could do anything. This felt too real to be an ordinary dream. John Hale promptly joined me amongst the mysterious white clouds.

"Try this," Hale said.

Fearlessly, he dove into a cloud. I followed him into the thick fog that made up the immaculate white cloud. It felt good, wet droplets spitting against my face. The golden white light from the sun hurt my eyes as I emerged. Man, I really dug flying. I still do, at middle age, in my dreams. It feels so good, so free, and always so real. John Hale taught me well.

"So Snyder," Hale looked at me as we shot past a screeching seagull, "don't you find it weird that we're both having the same dream at the same time?"

"I thought this was my dream."

"Well, it's my dream too. Isn't that obvious to you?

Hale was the smartest kid in the class.

"This is your dream?"

"No. It's our dream, Snyder. I read about this kind of thing in a psychology book."

"Flying?"

"No stupid, dual dreams. Two people sharing the same dream."

"How do I know you're not just part of my dream and the real John Hale isn't at home dreaming about the Green Bay Packers?"

"Simple solution, Snyder – ask me about the dream when you see me at school tomorrow."

John Hale spun left, executed a series of brisk rolls and spins before rocketing off into the horizon over the blue Pacific Ocean.

2.

"Rise and shine, Billy boy."

It was my mother's gentle voice.

Sitting up in my warm bed, I was completely awake, stunned over the reality of the dream. The taste of the salty ocean air was still on my lips.

Unlike most dreams, this one stayed with me. It had been so incredibly genuine, so palpable to all five of my senses. As I dressed for school, I wondered. And I kept wondering as my mother drove me to church, as I sat, stood, knelt, and genuflected through the six-thirty mass, as I ate my oatmeal with raisins and clumps of brown sugar at Chips Coffee Shop. Was it real? Heck yes it was real. I could still taste the salt and feel the moisture from the clouds. But would John Hale remember?

Hale showed up late to class. I tried to make eye contact but totally engrossed in the lessons of the day, he ignored me. Not only was he the undisputed smartest kid in the fourth grade, he was also Sister Agnes' pet. She didn't even get bent out of shape when he corrected her frequent multiplication and division errors as she worked out problems on the green blackboard. David Lopez once pointed out a mistake and she nearly beat him to death with a yard stick.

It was lunchtime. Hale was playing quarterback in a pickup game on the asphalt church parking lot that was our playground. Tony Frink made a picture perfect diving circus catch, tearing up his forearm on the asphalt. This was a common lunchtime injury. Tony's skin was raw from wrist to elbow. There was considerable amount of blood and sparkling chunks of black asphalt were imbedded into his arm. It was an honorable injury. Tony looked proudly at his impressive bloody wound and took his spot on the line of scrimmage. Hale glanced over at me. I was still staring, wondering if he was waiting for me to mention the incredible dream we had shared just hours before. He called time out and walked over to me.

"What the heck are you staring at?"

The kid was sweating. His glasses were fogged up. He took the glasses off and rubbed the lenses with his perfect white handkerchief.

"Well?"

"Well what?"

"Why do you keep staring at me, Snyder? Are you some kind of queer or something?"

His breath was pretty bad. This was the direct result of the liverwurst sandwich I had watched him eat for lunch.

"No, I'm not a queer!" I protested, "Listen, Hale, you didn't have any weird dreams last night, did you?"

"No."

"Come on Hale, quit wasting time. The bell's gonna ring."

It was Tony Frink, the sun reflecting miraculously from his heroic crimson wound.

"You ever fly in your dreams?"

"What the heck is wrong with you, Snyder?"

"I bet you don't remember your dreams, right?"

"You're weird, Snyder."

"Okay, I suppose you never read a book about dual dreams?"

"What are you talking about?"

"Have you?"

"No."

"Really?"

"Really."

"Okay."

"Quit staring, okay?"

"Okay."

Hale returned to his game and I quit staring. It was relatively clear that I had been wrong about the dual dream, but in the back of my mind, I wondered. The truth is I still wonder. John Hale and I would remain friends for the rest of his life. I respected him for his brains and his ability to play the drums. He was a talented drummer. He respected me for my ability to draw unimaginably intricate and bloody Civil War battle scenes. We went through a spoonerism phase in which he referred to me as *Snill Byder* and I called him *Hon Jale*. That's the kind of thing you do when you hang out with the smartest kid in the class. By the eighth grade, I began to notice that John would sometimes whisper to himself at his desk during religion class. He didn't do it often, but he did it enough for everyone to notice. Silently, he would mouth words, then shake his head and put his hands over his face. I don't know if he was praying, talking to himself, hearing voices or what. His classmates and the nuns ignored the behavior. John Hale was still a good guy, a smart guy and a respectable quarterback, even if he was a little different.

3.

I didn't have any classes with John our first two years at Hawthorne High. He took the college track classes while I stuck with the easy classes. He played football and I played basketball. Although we ran in different circles, I saw him around from time to time. After our sophomore year, we ended up in the same summer school driver's training class. The instructor was Mr. T – not to be confused with Rocky Balboa's pugilistic nemesis, our Mr. T was a Polish guy with a name nobody, not even Mr. T himself, could pronounce. Hailing from the East Coast, he was a funny guy. He used the old line, *don't assume anything because you'll make an ass of 'u' and 'me.'* Mr. T was a good teacher, one of the best. I still remember statistics he taught us, statistics such as seventy percent of all accidents happen less than a mile from home. He also taught us to watch out for women in curlers. Women don't really wear curlers anymore, but if I do happen to sec a woman driving with curlers in her hair, trust me, I'll be plenty wary.

Steven Spielberg's blockbuster *Jaws* came out that summer. John Hale lent me his paperback copy of the novel. That same day, he told me a pretty good joke. It stuck with me. The joke went something like this:

This guy goes on vacation and he asks his friend to watch his cat. After a couple of days, the guy calls his buddy.

"Hey man, how's my cat?"

His buddy says, "Your cat's dead, man."

"What?"

"I said your cat's dead, man."

"What the hell is wrong with you? You don't just tell a guy his cat's dead."

"Really? Why not?"

"It's too much of a shock. You have to ease into it. You might begin with something like, 'Your cat's on the roof.' And the next day you could say something like, 'The cat's at the vet.' And the third day, you might gently say, 'I'm sorry man, I don't know of any easy way to tell you this so I'm just going to tell you. The old cat didn't make it.' You've got to ease into it, see?"

"Yeah. I'm sorry, man."

"That's okay. So how's my mom doing?"

"Um, she's on the roof."

I thought this was just about the funniest joke I'd ever heard. I really went into hysterics. John Hale was a master when it came to telling a joke. He had an air of sophistication that was well above that of your average fifteen year-old and it added credibility to his delivery.

The next day, John Hale didn't make it to class. I had his copy of *Jaws*. I had burned through the novel in a single night. Rumors began to circulate. Unspeakable rumors. By the time I got home my mother confirmed them. John Hale had locked himself in a bathroom and shot and killed himself.

Everyone had a theory. It was over a girl. He was upset because James Solis beat him out for starting quarterback.

He was crazy. There must have been a dozen rumors. To this day, Tony Frink doesn't believe John Hale committed suicide.

"I was his lab partner in chemistry. I talked to him every day of our sophomore year and he was always talking about his plans to go to UCLA. It just doesn't make any sense."

That's what Tony will tell you. But they did find him in the bathroom with the door locked. What was he doing in the bathroom with the door locked and a loaded gun? I still had his book. Had his last joke been told to me? Had I been the last person to ever share a laugh with John Hale? Was the morbidity of the joke some kind of a hint or cry for help? Did I say or do something that contributed to his decision to take his own life, that is if he did purposely take his own life?

John was not my first experience with death, but he was my first experience with suicide. I still see John from time to time, in my dreams. He's usually just standing around off to the side when I catch him in my peripheral dream vision. We never talk. His effect on me has assuredly been profound. The religions of the world all seem to tell us that dreams have significance in our lives. I'd like to ask the John Hale of my dreams why he did it and why he keeps appearing in my dreams. The problem is I never know I'm dreaming when I dream about John Hale.

DART SAFETY AND THE PURPLE BIKINI

1971

Surfer Girl by Hawthorne's own Beach Boys played on the baby blue transistor radio my father had sent me for Christmas. Cary Blazejowski stood awkwardly in front of the opened garage door; I could barely see him for the onrush of late morning sunlight from behind. I was hanging out in the garage throwing darts. The truth is I spent a lot of time hanging out in that musty old garage that summer.

"Hey Billy, can I play with you?"

Cary was nine and I was eleven.

"I don't play, I hang out, you little geek," I unloaded on the goofy little kid.

Now I was plenty goofy myself and had experienced more than my share of derision from those my own age and even more from the older kids in the neighborhood, so it was nice to have someone I could shove around once in a while.

Cary sat on a sawhorse, watching me toss the darts. Feeling full of myself, I began to consider Mingo from *The Daniel Boone Show*, throwing knives and hatchets. Mingo's real name was Ed Ames and I'd seen him demonstrate his real life expertise with hatchet-throwing on the Johnny Carson Show earlier that week.

"Let me throw the darts, Billy."

"You're too young. Darts are dangerous and you could get hurt. Then it would be my responsibility."

"C'mon, I wanna play."

"Shut up and watch the master, you little dork."

Cary Blazejowski was more than grateful to retrieve the darts after I threw them. Feeling mighty confident after a few particularly good tosses, I was starting to picture myself in Mingo's league. Mingo was, without a doubt, the coolest guy on the Daniel Boone show, cooler than Rosie Greer or Daniel Boone. He was a bad-ass Indian dude who had been educated in England.

"Come on, Billy. Let me play."

It was pathetic.

"Okay."

A bad idea bubbled to the surface of my prepubescent mind. Picking up a flat, yellow carpenter's pencil, I shoved Cary over to the dartboard.

"Now, stick this pencil in your mouth."

"Put the pencil in my mouth?"

"Yeah, like a cigarette."

I was impatient.

"Oh, you're gonna knock the pencil outta my mouth with a dart like Mingo did with the hatchets on Johnny Carson!"

The kid was excited.

Shoving the pencil into his mouth, I backed up a few paces and picked out a dart.

"Yeah, that's it, Blazejowski. Now hold still."

The kid was shaking as I took careful aim.

"Are you sure you know how to do this, Billy?"

"Sure I'm sure, now hold still."

I was concentrating with everything I had. None too happy with what was going on, Kookie the Wonder Dog began to whimper at my feet.

"Shut up, Kookie. Can't you see I'm trying to concentrate here?"

Beads of sweat began to form on Cary Blazejowski's forehead as he struggled to hold still with his ear pressed against the dartboard. It was already hot. A prop plane buzzed low overhead. I took careful aim at the yellow pencil. The moist and salty ocean air caused the metal and plastic dart to feel slippery between my fingers. Squinting, I was one with Mingo. The smell of lawnmower gasoline, sawdust, spilled laundry detergent and the Pacific Ocean breeze filled my lungs as I took a deep breath. In one motion, I released the air and the dart, hard and smooth. The dart sailed across the garage.

Thwwwack.

"ARGHHH!" Blazejowski bellowed in sheer terror.

The dart had stuck to the side of Cary Blazejowski's skull and was reverberating back and forth.

"YOU KILLED ME! I'M GONNA DIE!" he screamed as he retreated down the concrete driveway. Kookie the Wonder Dog followed the kid, then turned to give me her *I told you so* look.

"Wait, Blazejowski!" I begged.

There was no waiting in this kid and I knew I was in big trouble. I sprinted after him as he hung a hard right at the end of the driveway. The plastic blue dart was bobbing up and down on the side of the kid's big head, looking very much like a matador's spear in the side of a bull.

Wait! Don't tell," I pleaded. "Please, Cary. I'll do anything you say. You can throw the darts."

"I CAN'T THROW DARTS, I'M BLEEDING TO DEATH!"

But he wasn't bleeding to death. As a matter of fact, I couldn't see any blood at all, just the blue dart bobbing up and down in coordination with his frantic strides. Blazejowski rounded the corner, heading east for his apartment building on Cranbrook Avenue. Cary was running and screaming like nobody's business with that silly dart bobbing up and down on the side of his head. I had to stop this kid from telling on me. I had to reason with him, but he was too fast.

By the time we reached Cary's apartment driveway, there were at least a dozen people behind me. Hot on my tail was Kookie the Wonder Dog. Behind Kookie was my nine year-old sister who had been watching the whole thing from the kitchen window. Behind my sister was Ali, our next-door neighbor from Iran, or as he constantly insisted, Persia. This guy was on top of everything that went down in the neighborhood. Creta, my summertime baby sitter, was bringing up the rear; I might interject that she was making great time for a woman of seventy. The scene reminded me of the story of the Gingerbread Man. I had to stop this kid from telling on me. He sprinted up the stairs, his screams echoing downward. A single, pinhead-sized, scarlet droplet glistened on the first of the chipped white stairs. I made it halfway up the stairway when I heard the rickety, aluminum screen door slam. Blood curdling screams reverberated down the stairway.

"What happened, Cary?"

It was Astrid, Cary's beautiful sixteen year-old sister. Just like every other red-blooded kid in the neighborhood, I was in love with Astrid Blazejowski.

"Billy Snyder threw a dart in Cary's head! I saw the whole thing!"

It was my sister standing behind me at the bottom of the stairs. She was taking this opportunity to exact revenge for a hundred or more injustices I had inflicted upon her.

Cary was still screaming like some kind of Malaysian tribesman run amuck. The screen door slammed again. Astrid appeared, like some Greek goddess, at the top of the white stairs holding a banana yellow Conair blow dryer. Never before had I seen such a hypnotic combination of pure beauty and rage. God, she was gorgeous. Her dishwater blond hair was short, yet full of thick womanly body. Astrid was a high school girl, practically a woman. And she was wearing a purple bikini. Don't ask me what in the wide world of sports she was doing in her apartment in a bikini. I don't know and it really doesn't matter. But Astrid Blazejowski was standing at the top of the paint-chipped stairs in a purple bikini. And she looked good to my eleven year-old eyes. Yes, she was the hottest thing I had ever seen. Without doubt, I was wearing a ridiculously perverted look as I gawked up from the bottom of the stairs.

"Did you throw that dart in my brother's head?"

My God, she was talking to me. I tried to think of something to say but nothing came to mind. I just stood there, ogling stupidly up at her.

"Yes!" More sweet revenge for my sister. "Billy did it! I saw the whole thing from the kitchen!"

Something in Astrid's eyes snapped me out of my goofball state of yearning and into some semblance of self-preservation, but it was too late. She was on me in a split second; grabbing hold of my white t-shirt, she slammed me against the cinder block wall. The force shocked me into a keener state of awareness. There were now dozens of people crowded into the driveway anxiously watching Astrid's retribution. Cary stood at the top of the stairs, above Astrid, tears cascading down his face, snot running from his nose and that stupid dart, still bobbing up and down from the side of his head.

The lovely Astrid Blazejowski commenced to give me the beating of my young life in that driveway on Cranbrook. She wailed on me as everyone who happened to be at home within eight city blocks had now crowded into that driveway to watch. She pummeled me girl-style, open-handed. When her hand became tired, she wailed on me with her plastic Conair until it shattered into a million pieces and she was holding nothing but a handle and a few dangling wires. Then she took off a rubber flip-flop and beat me over the head with it for what seemed several minutes. She continued to pound down on my head, face and shoulders until she was completely exhausted. And then Astrid Blazejowski stood before me, her beautiful hair soaked with sweat, her chest, covered with shimmering droplets of sweat, was heaving up and down, up and down, a flip-flop in one hand and the remnants of her ruined blow dryer in the other.

Dazed and bewildered, I was still wearing a stupid grin. My head and shoulders were throbbing. My face and ears stung. My eardrums were ringing. And I was feeling something else that my developing mind couldn't quite define. But I was pretty sure it felt good.

I stood there staring at her until she said, "Get out of here you goofy idiot."

I turned and staggered a few steps down the driveway before stopping and wheeling back for one last look. She was magnificent. Cary poked his head out from behind her bare hip. Wasn't anyone going to pull the dart from that poor, stupid kid's head?

"Get! Before I call the cops!"

Her shout blasted down the driveway and bounced around in my head.

Staggering, I made my way toward the street. My equilibrium was off. Awkwardly, I fell toward the wall.

"One step at a time," I thought as I kicked a Big Wheel out of my way.

The masses parted like the Red Sea and I struggled to move ahead. I was confused. Colors became indistinguishable. Everything faded to black and white. Dramatic music began to pound away in my head. I glanced at Ali the Iranian guy. He began to take on the appearance of Karl Malden. Losing my balance, I fell against the wall once again. A kid moved to help me.

"No!" Ali stopped him. "He has to do this by himself."

A half-smoked cigarette dangled from Ali's mouth. Heroically, I plodded along, lurching, battered but defiant, one step at a time, feeling oddly like Terry Malloy in the final scene of *On the Waterfront*.

THE SOUTH BAY DAILY BREEZE

1972

It is a hot summer day and I'm sitting on the front lawn with my dog Kookie, doing absolutely nothing. Greg Hotzenbueler rolls up in front of my house on his bad ass, cherry metal flake, three speed Schwinn Stingray. Hotzenbueler adroitly snatches a newspaper from the loaded canvas bags and expertly zings it to the doormat. At fourteen, Hotzenbueler is a couple of years older than me. Every once in a while he takes a break from his paper route to wrestle me. He generally whoops up on me three or four times before getting back on his Stingray and finishing his route. What might it be like, I wonder, to be as cool as Greg Hotzenbueler? Sitting in the driveway, he bestows me with a blank stare.

"Hi, Hotzenbueler," I say.

"Hey, Snyder," he says, the blank look still just hanging around.

"You want to kick my ass in wrestling again?"

"No, it's too hot. Hey, you want my paper route?"

There is no need to think about it. A kid like me doesn't say no to a kid like Greg Hotzenbueler. The very next day, Hotzenbueler is instructing me on the intricacies of delivering the newspaper for the South Bay Daily Breeze. He teaches me the triple fold method and advises me to place forty or fifty rubber bands around my wrist in order to increase speed. Once the canvas bags are loaded onto my spray painted, orange, Sears knockoff of a Schwinn Stingray, he guides me through the route. Hotzenbueler teaches me to hold the paper with the thumb and index finger, resting it on the shoulder, right next to the ear, before slinging it onto the customer's porch. It isn't long before I hit a bump in the street, the heavy paper bags pull the back wheel off the ground and my bicycle does a flip, propelling me through the air. I am a screaming prepubescent projectile. My flight ends in the brittle hedges in front of Astrid Blazejowski's apartment building.

"Whatever you do Snyder, don't quit this route until after Christmas. Last year I made sixty bucks in Christmas tips. That's how I bought this here Stingray."

Within a few days, I have this paper route routine down. Resolved that I will not quit at least until January, I become serious about the business of delivering papers. Collecting payment at the end of the month is the trickiest part of the job. Customers are often grouchy, even mean. Sometimes they move away and I am stuck with the bill. The pay is not good, three bucks for a good month – and that includes tips. My first month, I have to fork over sixty-five cents out of my own pocket. But I know my labor will rewarded when Christmas-time rolls around. I've already got my bad ass, banana yellow, three speed Schwinn Stingray picked out at Phil's Bike shop.

Sunday is the best and worst day when it comes to delivering papers. Of course getting up at 4:30 in the morning is a grueling endeavor for a twelve year-old. It's cold outside and the Sunday paper is five times heavier and bulkier than the weekly paper. There are Sundays when I have to come back to the house to reload my bags. And it's not easy steering a bike with two hundred pounds of newspapers sagging from the handlebars. I live with the knowledge that one pebble can catapult me into the thorny hedges in front of Astrid Blazejowski's apartment building.

My grandfather's dog Pepper comes with me on Sundays. Don't ask me why she comes with me, she just does. Pepper is a cockapoo. Everyone seems to have a cockapoo these days; they are ubiquitously stylish, like zucchini and Hamburger Helper. The first Sunday I delivered papers, Pepper escaped from my grandfather's bachelor apartment in the back yard. I tried catching her but those cockapoos are deceptively fast. It was too early and I was too tired. The dog raced along at my side as I threw my papers; it was as if she'd been doing it her entire life. Now it's business as usual. There is no one out on Sunday mornings – except the kid that delivers the Herald Examiner and the old lady with cat's eye glasses and curlers that delivers the L.A. Times from her old Buick. It feels good, like I'm in charge just one time a week – just the dog, the papers, and me. The further I go, the lighter the bag; the lighter the bag the faster I go – just me, the papers and the dog. It feels real good, especially when I throw that last paper, knowing that in five minutes I'll be warm between the sheets of my own bed.

It's the day after Thanksgiving, the day the Christmas lights go up. And this year, because I am twelve, my mother has given me the go ahead to hang the lights myself. Somewhere in excess of two hours have been spent spent untangling the green cords. The lights have been checked and the bad bulbs replaced. The nails have been firmly placed in the wood trim since we moved into the house five years ago. Baby, believe me when I tell you I'm ready to hang some Christmas lights. With the lights wrapped urbanely around my bony shoulder, I step onto the aluminum ladder, envisioning myself to be some death defying Army Ranger, ascending the treacherous cliffs of Monte Cassino. Safely on the roof, I begin to work the light cord around the nails. My left hand slips on the grey roofing and gravity pulls me off balance. My adrenalin kicks in and my heart rate quickens as I regain my footing. The last thing I want to do is fall off of this roof and break my arm. Those Christmas tips will be piling in next month and that bad ass, banana yellow, three speed Schwinn Stingray is waiting for me behind the plate glass window at Phil's Bike Shop. My heart rate approaches normalcy as I wrap the light cord around another nail.

"Good morning, William."

It is Johnny Torres standing at the bottom of the ladder. This kid is one of a kind. At the ripe old age of eleven, he has the voice of a fifty-seven year-old truck driver. It's really strange; the kid is undersized for his age but he possesses freakishly mature facial features. He looks a little like Edward G. Robinson. Johnny Torres is the neighborhood wheeler and dealer. On Sundays, he sets out from paper machine to paper machine, dropping in a quarter and cleaning them out, one by one. Then he stands in front of the church selling his stolen Sunday papers to the parishioners as they leave mass. In the past he's offered to help me rake leaves or mow the lawn, out of the goodness of his own heart, then gone to my mother and demanded payment. This kid is trouble with a capital Torres.

"What do you want, Torres?" I ask warily.

"Nothing. I don't want nothing at all, Billy. What are you doing up there?" he asks with his hands shoved deep into his pockets.

"I'm stealing papers to sell at church. Now get the heck out of here, Torres." I sneer in my most spiteful voice.

"I'll help you. I don't got nothing else to do, Billy," he says, sounding something like Lurch from *The Adams Family*.

"Yeah, I don't need your kind of help. Now get the heck out of here."

He defiantly places the toe of his tattered PF Flier on the bottom step of the ladder.

"What are you doing down there, Torres?"

"I told you Billy, I want to help you."

"And I told you Torres, I don't want your kind of help."

Torres takes hold of the ladder as I shout, "Don't come up here. If you fall, you could sue my mother."

"I won't sue your mother. Just let me watch."

It becomes evident that he plans on coming up no matter what I say when he tightens his grip and places a PF Flyer on the second step of the ladder.

Grabbing hold of the cold aluminum at top of the ladder, I shout, "I said don't come up here, Torres!"

He takes a second step and quite brilliantly, I take firm hold and shove the ladder with both hands. Torres steps down and the ladder flips over him – pulling me forward, still hanging onto the top like some out-of-control pole-vaulter. It feels very much like I am flying, for just that split second before I come crashing, wrists first, to the front lawn. There is the sound of bones in my wrists popping and snapping. Strangely, I feel nothing at all – for about a second and a half. And then the white pain explodes like a crashing freight train. I scream in window rattling anguish and the slightest movement makes the excruciating torture even more excruciating. My hands hang from my wrists like a couple of broken chicken necks.

Torres stands over me and asks in his freakishly low voice, "What the heck did you do that for, Billy?"

To which I reply, "Arghhh, my arms! I broke my arms!" and then I remember, "There goes my banana yellow, three speed Stingray."

My mother bursts from the screen door and promptly tells me to shut up. She doesn't believe me until the two-bit criminal from around the corner confirms in his Lou Rawls voice that I have indeed plummeted, palms first, from the roof. He assures her that he indeed did hear the bones crack.

My mother screams at me for falling off the roof during the entire ride to the emergency room. Somehow the Munchkin version of Paul Robson has talked my mother into letting him come along. At the emergency room, I cannot, no matter how hard I try, get a word in edge wise as Torres explains in great detail how I fell from the roof. The doctor shushes me when I demand to be allowed to give my side of the story. The doctor is fascinated with Torres' creepy voice.

"Exactly how long has it been since your voice changed, young man?" marvels the doctor.

"My voice ain't changed," Torres bellows.

"You mean you've always sounded like this?"

"That's right, doc."

"This is absolutely fascinating. Would you mind waiting right here while I get the other doctors?"

"What about my arm?" I demand.

I abscond from the emergency room with my broken wrist in a cast and my sprained wrist in a sling. The next day, there is a knock at the front door. It is Torres. He explains that under the darkness of night, like some kind of demented Christmas light elf, he has taken it upon himself to hang the lights. When my mother asks if she can pay him, he says the charge is ten bucks – cash. Upon collecting ten crisp ones, he gloats that the doctor gave him a card and UCLA Medical Center is going to pay him sixty dollars to scrutinize his vocal chords. The good news is I won't have to do any writing in school for at least a month. Of course the bad news is I'll have to give up the paper route. Frank Louder graciously agrees to take over for me. Frank will collect my Christmas tips; there will be no banana yellow Stingray. Is there no justice in this world? All I can say is I hope you're satisfied wherever you are, Mr. Johnny Torres.

THE KURT SMART STORIES

1972-1977

1972

Kurt Smart was a wiry kid with brush cleaner hair and more than his share of freckles. I don't quite remember how or when we became friends, but I am amazed that we remained friends as long as we did. Kurt was a good guy, smart with a good sense of humor, and we enjoyed each other's company or I should state that I enjoyed his company. I'll be doggoned if I wasn't some kind of walking voodoo curse on the poor kid.

My grandfather, who lived in the back house, worked in a pumpkin lot every October, and he made it his responsibility to bring home an enormous pumpkin more enormous than the one he had brought home the previous year. When I was twelve, I came home from school to find a pumpkin the size of a Volkswagen sitting atop the red stained picnic table on the backyard patio. Filled with pure exhilaration, I rushed into my grandfather's apartment.

"It's the biggest stinkin' pumpkin I ever saw. Can I carve it?"

"What else were you thinkin' of doin' with it, ya dumb-ass? Were you gonna play checkers with the damned thing?"

"Can I use the knives?"

He shot me his *you're an idiot* look. Believe me when I tell you I'd seen that look before. Snatching up a handful of razor-sharp knives, I sprinted clumsily back out to the flag-stone patio while my grandfather sat in his easy chair chain smoking non-filtered Camels and watching Chick Hearn's *Bowling for Dollars*. Now, I've got a pretty good idea of what you're thinking. He let a twelve-year-old run out the door with a handful of sharp knives?

Yes he did. My grandfather was not known for his ability to keep children out of trouble. I have been told that one of my uncles set the back lawn on fire three times on one afternoon while my grandfather sat right next to him in a lawn chair, smoking Camels, drinking Olympia beer and listening to Vin Scully call the Dodger game on his transistor radio.

I was geared up for pumpkin surgery with the six very sharp knives laid out before me when Kurt Smart hopped gracefully over the fence and into the back yard.

"Holy crap, Billy! Where the heck did you get that thing?"

Kurt was impressed.

"Spaceship dropped it off this morning."

I suppose I thought I was pretty smart. Picking up a razor sharp knife that must have been two feet long, I began to toss it from hand to hand.

Tauntingly, I sang.

"When you're a Jet, you're a Jet you're a Jet, from your first livin' breath to your last cigarette. Da-na-na-na-nah!"

"Better be careful with that thing, man," Kurt said.

"Don't you worry about me, Smart; I know how to handle a blade."

Summarily, I got down to the business of slicing and dicing. After carving open a lid, Kurt and I reached down deep into the orange monster, pulled up thousands of slippery pumpkin seeds and spread them out on a sheet of newspaper. Later we would salt and bake them. Pumpkin seeds were darned near as good as sunflower seeds.

Kurt begged me to let him do some slicing and dicing of his own. Ignoring his desperate pleas, I carved out the eyes. I felt the power. I had that razor sharp knife and Kurt Smart wanted it.

"Slow down, Smart. I'll let you try in a minute," I said, slowly stringing him along.

By the time I finished up the nose, the poor kid had nearly reached the point of hysteria.

"Come on, Billy; let me give it a shot."

The gigantic knife hung low at my side, the blade pointed at Kurt. God only knows why, but Kurt made a sudden move for the blade. Instinctively, I pulled the knife away. What followed was perhaps, for want of more descriptive terminology, the ickiest sound I have ever heard. As his hand closed in around the deadly blade, I heard the sound of the razor sharp metal scraping against the raw white bone where Kurt's index finger and thumb bones met. Heebie-jeebie chills raced up and down my spine. The sound was worse than that of a thousand fingernails scraping on a thousand chalkboards. Gallons of crimson blood cascaded from Kurt's hand and splashed upward from the faded pink flagstone patio as he stood with a blank look of shock on his colorless freckled face.

"You cut my hand open, Billy," Kurt muttered blankly.

I'm guessing he was in clinical shock. In an instant, there was screaming, running and general confusion. This was the one and only time I would ever have the opportunity to watch my grandfather run. He moved darned well for a chain-smoking, hard-drinking, easy chair-sitting grandfather. We stopped the bleeding with a pair of my grandfather's size fifty, Fruit of the Loom jockey shorts that had been conveniently hanging on the clothesline. Kurt's mother did get him to the hospital before he bled to death. Strangely enough, I didn't get into any serious trouble over the ordeal. After all, Kurt had grabbed the deadly blade and pulling back was a natural reaction.

When I saw Kurt the next day, his hand was wrapped in clinical gauze. He looked like he was wearing a giant white boxing glove. It looked kind of funny – so I chuckled, just a little bit, but enough for Kurt to notice.

"That's some kind of bandage you have there, Kurt."

Kurt stared at me, making it a point to say absolutely nothing.

"Hey man, I'm sorry, Kurt."

"No, you're not," Kurt snapped back.

This would not be the last time the two of us would exchange these phrases. I got Kurt's point. I mean what kind of friend was I? Less than twenty-four hours earlier I had almost sliced the boy's hand off and now I was laughing about it?

1974

A couple of years had passed and all had been forgotten. At least I had forgotten. Kurt showed up in my drive way, dragging a rusted old basketball hoop. The two of us decided we would hang it above the garage door. We dug up an old rectangular sheet of badly warped plywood in the garage and devised a simple plan. First, we would nail the plywood to the support two-by-fours that jutted out from below the roof. Then we would brace the backboard to the roof with more two-by-fours. Using the six-foot cinder block wall right next to the garage, I scampered effortlessly onto the roof. Kurt leaned an aluminum ladder against the garage and climbed up, carefully balancing the hunk of warped plywood that would be our backboard above his head. I grabbed hold of the plywood. My grandfather stepped out of his apartment, Camel non-filter braced firmly between his teeth, and surveyed the situation.

"What the hell are you two mallet heads doin'?"

As I turned to look down at my grandfather, I let go of the plywood.

"We're hanging up a basketball hoop, Grandpa."

Of course when I let go Kurt was sucked off balance with such force that he flipped backward and fell to the concrete driveway fast and hard. It honestly looked like something directly out of a Roadrunner cartoon. When Kurt let out a slow groan, there was nothing I could do but laugh. It was one of those *you're not supposed to laugh in church* laughs. Here was this poor kid sprawled out on the concrete driveway, the wind knocked out of his lungs, moaning and groaning and I was up on the roof absolutely laughing my ass off. He could have been seriously injured. But he wasn't seriously injured, so it really was pretty funny – from where I was standing, on top of the roof and what not. All I could do was look at my down-on-his-luck friend lying flat on the concrete with his arms extended above his shoulders, still holding that ridiculous warped hunk of plywood over his head, looking just exactly like Wile E. Coyote, and laugh my ass off.

1976

Although we began to move in different circles, Kurt and I remained friends through the high school years. My focus moved to the basketball court while Kurt's focus shifted to teenage romance. Kurt worked every summer as a counselor up in the mountains at Hawthorne Youth Camp where he went by the camp name of Wookie. He was heavily into the Star Wars, Hobbit, and fantasy novel business. I feel compelled to make it clear that Kurt was the most down to earth guy I've ever known who was involved in that particular circuit. I suppose it was before the Star Trek, Star Wars, and Hobbit set took a turn for the kooky and obsessive side. At any rate, Kurt hooked up with a cute blonde during the summer between his freshman and sophomore years. Her parents were the camp caretakers, and the family lived up in the mountains year round. Kurt walked around in a lovesick haze until the two were married a couple of weeks after graduation. Last I heard, they had three beautiful girls who are now young adults, and against all young marriage odds, Kurt and his wife are still together.

My first girlfriend was Patty Nelson. She was one of Kurt's fellow camp counselors. Patty was a good-looking blonde softball player who went to school across town at Adolph Leuzinger High. Is that a great name for a high school or what? I never really got to know much about her. Our relationship consisted of me picking her up from work at Baskin-Robbins Ice Cream Shop at ten and getting her home by ten-fifteen every Monday, Tuesday, and Thursday night. Her grandfather didn't allow her to hang out or go to parties or date, and I don't think he knew she was calling me her boyfriend. I could be sure that grandpa would be waiting on the porch, smoking a fat cigar, and appearing somewhat dangerous when I dropped her off from the ice cream joint. Looking back, the old guy bore a strong resemblance to Ernest Hemingway. My first encounter with romance lasted just a couple of months. We did go to a school dance and see the movie *Saturday Night Fever* together. I can count the number of times we engaged in some form of actual lip lock on one hand. She didn't want me hanging out and going to parties without her, so I hung out with Kurt – a lot.

One Saturday night we were sitting around at my house playing Monopoly. I was sixteen, with a driver's license and I was playing Monopoly with Kurt, Tracy Turner, Fred Torres, and get this, my mother. Tracy was also a Hawthorne Youth Camp counselor; he went by the camp name Ziggy, since he was disturbingly into David Bowie. He used to play his guitar and sing Bowie songs. The guy probably had the worst singing voice I'd ever heard, and he had this habit of looking you in the eye when he sang. This staring and singing combination really gave me the willies. Tracy was a superior athlete. He was six-six, weighed two twenty-five, and played football, basketball, and baseball. As a six-six, left-handed pitcher, he was being actively pursued by the major leagues.

The third Monopoly player was Fred Torres. I have never known anyone even remotely like Fred. Coming from a terrible family situation, he created a distinctive persona for himself, wearing thick glasses with a suit and tie to parties populated by kids in t-shirts, O.P. shorts and flip-flops. Utilizing his unique senses of humor and style, he managed to keep company with the most beautiful girls at school, Faline Kline, Shelly McCarrol and Dayleen Barrientos, just to name a few. I don't think there was any making out involved, but Fred's relationships with these girls were symbiotic in that he made them laugh and they made Fred look good.

So there we were playing Monopoly on a Saturday night. I was bored out of my skull when the phone rang. I answered and on the other end of the line was the love of my young life. Making a mad dash to my bedroom, I took the call on the second line.

"Okay, Patty. You there?"

"I miss you."

"I miss you too."

"We miss you too, Billy"

They were on the other line in the kitchen.

I rushed to the kitchen, breathing fire.

"Knock it off or I swear I'll get you all back. You too, Mom!"

My own mother was in on this childishness. Trotting back to the bedroom, I plopped down on my by bed and picked up the phone. After much inane babbling, Patty dropped a nuclear bomb.

"We have to break up, Billy."

"What? Hold on!"

The idiots and my mom were guffawing in the hallway.

"We have to break up with you too, Billy."

They were merciless.

Pulling the door open, I let Tracy have it right between the eyes with one of my size twelve, Nike basketball shoes. They scattered like so many pigeons.

"Hello."

"Yes."

She was whispering.

"Why are you whispering?"

"I'm not supposed to be on the phone after ten. Just listen, I can't explain any better than this."

There was nothing.

"Hello!"

I was dying inside.

There was the sound of a record needle, some scratching and then:

Don't go changing to try and please me.
Don't change the color of your hair.

My God, she was playing a Billy Joel record in order to break up with me. There were screams of laughter coming from the kitchen.

And then, "I just want someone – that I can talk to, I love you just the way you arrrre!"

They were singing along again. This was getting old.

I yelled into the phone, "Hang up you jerks! …Hello, Patty! Are you there?"

There was nothing but that stupid Billy Joel song. Right then and there, the epiphany hit – and I didn't even know what the hell an epiphany was. I saw the light, the absurdity of Patty's sappy break up song, the absurdity of this whole silly relationship. I opened the bedroom door and watched the three goofballs and my mom falling over the kitchen table, spilling popcorn, hysterically laughing and singing, Fred in his coat and tie, the wavy red imprints from the rubber sole of my Nike on Tracy Turner's forehead, and my mother struggling with all of her might not to laugh when she saw me.

A couple of hours passed. My mother had gone to bed, *Saturday Night Live* was over, and Peter Frampton was performing on *Don Kushner's Rock Concert*. We were playing Yahtzee as Larry, Curly, and Mo were just finishing their one hundred seventy-fourth rendition of *I Love You Just the Way You Are*. I was holding a pepper shaker in my hand. I looked at the pepper shaker. I was bored. I was tired. I was embarrassed. I was angry.

Looking at the pepper shaker, I wondered if blowing pepper in someone's face would really make them sneeze, like in the Three Stooges movies.

Why not? I thought.

The three tenors began to drown out Peter Frampton's *Ooh Baby I Love Your Way* with that horrible monotonous Billy Joel song. Sprinkling a little pepper into the palm of my hand, I held it to my mouth, turned to Kurt who was singing joyfully and … poof. I blew.

Kurt did not sneeze like the characters in Three Stooges movies. Instead, he placed his palms over his eyes and fell to the floor where he writhed in pain and screamed in agony.

"AHHHHHHHHH! MY EYES!"

Kurt Smart wriggled and bellowed on the floor like he was dying for a couple of minutes. And what did I do? The same thing I did when he crashed to the concrete driveway with a hunk of plywood over his head, the same thing I did when I saw his hand wrapped in that giant boxing glove, I laughed. Not out loud boisterous laughing, but that *trying to hold it in during church* kind of laughing. I don't know why. Laughing is a funny thing. I knew then as I know now that it's a hell of thing to blow pepper in your friend's eyes, causing him fall to the floor, writhing and screaming in pain. Even after he'd been one of the guys who had humiliated me while my first girlfriend was breaking up with me on the phone, it was still a hell of a thing. But it was pretty funny. Even as I was handing him a glass of water to splash in his eyes to relieve the pain, I looked at his beet red eyes and fought hopelessly to hold back laughter.

Patty and I were finished. Other girls would come along to break my heart again and again. Kurt and I did not speak for at least a month. When I passed him at school, I tried to say something, but I kept breaking out in laughter instead. I don't understand it, but I do know it's a hell of a thing to laugh at a friend after slicing his hand open, or causing him to fall off of a ladder and crash into the concrete, or even blowing pepper in his eyes.

It's a hell of a thing.

HOOPS

1973-1978

It was 1977. I was executing layup drills with the Hawthorne Cougars varsity basketball team at the El Camino Community College gym. Lay-up drills were cool. It felt good to catch the leather ball, take two strong dribbles, leap hard from the smooth hardwood floor, bringing my hand up over the rim and drop the ball into the basket. I couldn't slam dunk, but I could get up and over that rim. Only Francis Bernard Rodriguez and the three Agee brothers could dunk the ball for our team.

Warming up on the other side of the court were the Morningside High School Monarchs. Everybody knew it was a sign of weakness to watch the opposing team warm up, so I tried not to look as each of the Morningside players demonstrated the ability to dunk the ball with explosive ferocity.

Byron Scott was over there warming up with the Monarchs. I'm talking about the same Byron Scott who coaches in the NBA, the same Byron Scott who starred for the Showtime Lakers, and the same Byron Scott who starred for the finest basketball team Arizona State ever put on the floor. And I am here to tell you that I guarded Byron Scott on that hot summer night.

Before the game, Coach Stucker took me aside and said, "Billy, I want you to stick Scott tonight."

"But I'm a forward and he's a guard."

"I know what I'm doing. You just stick to that kid like a cheap suit and stay stuck. I want you to be able to tell me what kind of gum he chews. He goes in the paint, you go in the paint. He goes outside, you go outside. He goes to the can, you go to the can. You got it?"

"Sure coach."

And I did stick to Byron Scott that night. It was me, the kid who was destined to become a beaten down school teacher; I stuck with Byron Scott, the kid who was destined to become a basketball superstar. On that night, our vastly differing fates did not matter. We were just a couple of finely tuned athletes gutting it out on the hardwood, hombre against hombre. And on that hot summer night, I did hold Byron Scott. I held him to seventy-seven points. And this was before the three point rule had been instituted. Byron Scott broke the El Camino Summer League scoring record with me guarding him. I honestly believe his seventy-seven-point performance gave his confidence a jolt. One can only wonder if he would have developed the self-assurance to go on to accomplish college and NBA greatness if it hadn't been for my defensive effort on that hot summer night. As for me, I would not again experience this kind of humiliation until the night of my senior prom.

Basketball is an important part of who I am. Well into middle age, I can still put the ball in the hole – if I need to. I suppose I have been playing, coaching and officiating basketball for more than three decades.

My sporting career began as a little league baseball player in first grade. Absolutely stinking up the field, I hated the game and was terrified of the ball, failing to chalk up even one hit the over the course of the entire season. My fear of the ball began on the first day of practice when the coach cracked me in the nose with an under arm pitch, releasing a steady flow of blood from my left nostril. My mother started offering me a quarter for a base hit. By the end of the season, she was up to five bucks. She could have safely offered five thousand. I played left field and the ball was hit in my direction just once. I acted like I didn't see it until the third basemen got underneath the fly ball. At that point, I felt safe to jog toward the ball and feign disappointment when the other kid called for the catch.

A second year with the WILCON Dodgers yielded no improvement. Mercifully, my mother did not pressure me to play another year. I think we both accepted the fact that I was not an athlete. As the second tallest kid in the class, people often asked if I played basketball. When I grew five inches over the summer between seventh and eighth grade, reaching six feet two inches in height, I decided to try out for the Saint Joseph's Parish School basketball team.

Standing more than six feet tall in the eighth grade was enjoyable for me. I was suddenly taller than most adults. People were saying things like, "Man stretch, you're tall," and "How's the weather up there?" I absolutely devoured the attention. My balance and coordination took some time to catch up with my growth spurt. Simple tasks like walking up stairs had become a formidable challenge.

The first adult book I read was *Foul,* the Connie Hawkins story. The paperback had been making its way around the boys in popular reading class because the dialogue contained so much colorful street lingo. Hawkins was an NBA superstar who had grown up in Harlem. I strongly identified with the Hawk, even though I did not, nor would I ever exhibit extraordinary talent.

I also identified with seven-foot-two-inch Wilt Chamberlain, who was playing out his final season with the Lakers. My most prized possession was a gold headband just like The Big Dipper's, thick across the forehead and narrow where it wrapped around the back. I wore that ridiculous thing around town every day. At six-two and a hundred pounds, with all of my pants riding four inches above my shoes, I must have cut a swashbuckling figure with that bright yellow headband stretched across my forehead.

Tryouts were held during the Christmas break at the basketball courts in the church parking lot. When my mother took me shopping for basketball shoes, I picked out a pair of green canvas Chuck Taylor All-Stars. They went quite nicely with the navy blue and gold school uniform. Although the most basic weave drills and dribbling exercises were utterly impossible for me to perform with any semblance of accomplishment and my knees and elbows were soon scraped and bruised from frequent falls on the hard, black asphalt, I found the tryouts electrifying.

The games were held at Father Junipero Serra High School in Gardena. Sitting in the stands before my first organized game, I savored the smell of the gym, the sound of shoes screeching on the wood floor, the piercing bursts from referees' whistles, the reverberation of the bouncing leather ball, and the deafening blast of the hand-held air horn at the scorers' table. My heart pounded wildly as I lined up for my first center jump. The opposing center, a white kid a couple of inches shorter than me, offered me the original soul brother handshake. We ceremoniously partook in the process. The ref tossed the ball and I won the tip. Shocked into paralysis, I stood at the center court line as Pat Rodriguez dribbled to the hoop and softly laid the ball in for the first two points of the game. Before it was over, I had grabbed a few rebounds and blocked a couple of shots. Although I possessed the coordination of a tangled garden hose, I had experienced more success in that first game than in two years of Little League. I was hooked.

The neighborhood game took place every day after school on my backyard court. As is true with all backyard courts, there were special rules. It was perfectly legal to slam opposing players into the metal garage door, making Kevin McNamara, who was three years older and at least forty pounds heavier than any of the rest of us, the court MVP. This garage door-checking rule made for an exceptionally loud game. It was also considered fair play to jump off of the metal garage door in order to dunk the ball. This was not always a very smart thing to do, especially if McNamara was on the opposing team. Then there was the low hanging telephone wire that stretched across the court. One had to factor that wire in when choosing where to launch shots. Whenever the wire stopped a shot, Jerry Pearl, a kid who went by the name of Preacher, would shout, "Blocked by the hand of the Lord!"

Preacher was my first black friend. He was a tremendous athlete, fast as lightening. He used to say he was so quick, he could flip off the light switch and be in bed before it was dark. Basketball was his game, but he excelled at everything he tried. Just for the heck of it, he ran cross-country his freshman year. When the season ended, he had set several school records. Some boxing coach got hold of him one summer. Preacher trained for a month before absolutely annihilating his opponent, a tough looking Mexican kid from East L.A. with a professional looking robe, trainer and entourage. He stopped boxing when the trainer asked him to skip the basketball summer league. Like I said, basketball was his game.

Looking back at my childhood, my family didn't have much money. I felt put upon because I was the only kid who couldn't buy lunch at McDonalds after drum corps parades. Instead, my mother packed me a brown bag with a peanut butter sandwich, an apple and a banana flavored Scooter Pie. Don't get me wrong, my mother worked hard to provide for my sister and me and for that I am eternally grateful. It's just that it was tough to smell those French fries and hear kids slurping chocolate shakes through straws while I was chomping on peanut butter and jelly. When the weather got cold, I wore my grandfather's old jacket with sleeves that stopped at my elbows. My mother slept on a pullout couch in the living room so my sister and I could have our own bedrooms. My humble teacher's salary allows my children to enjoy a standard of living that far exceeds that of my childhood.

Preacher's family was poor. I lived in a furnished house while Preacher lived in an unfurnished apartment. When I say unfurnished I mean there was no furniture. Preacher shared one of the two bedrooms with several kids. Everybody slept on the floor. Piles of clothes were scattered across the room. Their refrigerator was usually empty, a concept that absolutely blew my mind. We always had something to eat; as a matter of fact, we had steaks every Sunday thanks to my Uncle Jack, who owned a butcher shop in Watts. They did have a color television set. I can remember waiting for Preacher to get ready to play basketball on Saturday mornings, sitting on the floor with Sammy, his nine-year-old nephew, watching Don Cornelius host *Soul Train*.

Preacher's mother and stepfather dropped us off to watch a double feature in downtown L.A. on a Saturday night. The first movie was *Enter the Dragon,* starring Bruce Lee, Jim Kelly and John Saxon. This was my first exposure to Bruce Lee. I was thunderstruck; the guy was so smooth, so quick and so damned cool. The second feature was *Thunderbolt and Lightfoot* with Clint Eastwood and Jeff Bridges.

It's funny, I can't imagine sitting in a movie theater over the course of a four hour double feature today and I certainly can't imagine a modern day fifteen year-old with that kind of staying power. About halfway through the Clint

Eastwood movie, Preacher, to my left, had his head tilted back on the seat and was snoring like a buzz saw. Preacher's sister Gertrude sat to my right. A year younger than me, Gertrude was at least six feet tall and put together like a Panzer tank. Who knows what got into her, but she started feeling amorous.

"Hey, Snyder."

Gertrude elbowed me hard in the ribs, making no attempt to keep her voice down.

"What?"

I kept my eyes on the screen.

"Snyder, give me a kiss."

No subtlety in this girl. I kept my eyes dead ahead, zeroed in on the big screen. She rammed her elbow into my ribs again – hard.

"Don't act like you don't hear me. Give me a kiss, Snyder!"

She was getting louder.

Panic began to set in. Looking around, I focused on the fact that I was the only white person in the theater. I had never been around this many black people. This girl wasn't going to let up.

"Hey Preacher," I whispered. "Wake up, man."

Gertrude's fist slammed into my shoulder. This time she had pulled off all the stops. Before I had time to react, she had nailed my shoulder with a second, solid shot.

"Why you talkin' to him, Snyder? He asleep. Now lemme have that kiss!"

No way was I going to kiss this girl. I continued to nudge Preacher and his terrorist sister continued to slam her fist into my arm and shoulder for what seemed like hours.

"Hey, Snyder, why don't you just do us all a favor and give that girl a kiss?"

I turned around. It was some guy with a *Link from the Mod Squad-style* Afro a few rows back.

When the lights finally came on I gave praise to God in Heaven and nudged Preacher, waking him up. There was no feeling in my right arm. Gertrude glared at me with murder in her eyes.

"You just a punk, Snyder. Scared to kiss a girl," Gertrude snarled.

I made a resolution to steer clear of Preacher's place for a while. My right arm dangled lifelessly as we waited on Preacher's parents outside the theater for what seemed to be another eternity. When the parents finally showed up, Preacher asked them why they were so late.

"Boy, don't you question me. I had some man's business that ain't none of your business!"

"I have to get up and do my paper route!"

"Boy, don't you cry to me about no silly ass paper route!"

"It's my job."

"You don't know nothin' about no job. You don't pay for no food or nothin'."

"I do too. I buy Sammy somthin' to eat every morning. If I didn't, he wouldn't eat."

"Boy, you shut your punk-ass mouth before I come back and beat your ass right in front of your little friend!"

We rode home in silence. I was almost thankful for the throbbing in my shoulder because it helped me escape the ugliness of the moment.

Preacher was a good friend. We played freshman ball together. He started while I rode the pine. He was always trying to help me out, feeding me the ball for scoring opportunities when he could. Freshman ball was a tough experience. Warming the bench did not sit well with me. My mother came to every home game. She was usually the only parent in the stands and there I was collecting splinters.

Looking back, I belonged on the bench. I was slow, weak, uncoordinated and entirely too timid. The coach was Barry Dean. He was everything that I was not: quick, strong, agile, aggressive and confident. Dean tried to teach me but I was completely scatterbrained.

The first time I got into a game and found myself with the ball in my hands, I forgot all about the plays. I was positioned at the top of the key. When my opponent got close up on me and started jabbing at the ball, I panicked. Another opponent dropped off on me for a double team. All I wanted to do was get rid of the ball. So I threw up a silly-ass hook shot that actually hit the rim. Everybody in the gym laughed. My face became hot and I felt tears welling up. The coach kept me on the bench for the next few games. My frustration grew; I couldn't sleep or concentrate on my school work. Sitting in the locker room after failing to make it off of the bench in a tournament game up on the Palos Verdes Peninsula, I stared down at my Chuck Taylors. The team was celebrating a victory, but I was trying to control the lump in my throat and the tears welling up in my eyes.

"What the hell's a matter with you, Snid?" one of the players quipped. "You're actin' like we lost."

That did it for me. I beat it out of the locker room and ran down the hallway. There was no controlling the onrush of tears. Rounding a corner, I took a seat in front of a classroom. Crying like hell, my chest was heaving, and my nose was running. There was no stopping it. I heard Preacher calling my name from around the corner. My pride was already crushed. The last thing I needed was for my teammates to see me bawling like a big pansy. I was able to stifle my sobs until Preacher's shouts faded into silence. The tears of frustration cascaded endlessly down my face.

At some point, Coach Dean wandered around the corner. He looked down at me. Barry Dean was a tough son of a bitch. He was a guy I wanted to impress. The coach knew I was uncoordinated; he knew I couldn't remember the plays; he knew I was physically weak, and now he knew that I couldn't handle things without crying like a God damned girl. But I couldn't stop.

"Where the hell you been? And what are you cryin' for?"

All I could do was cover my face. Dean grabbed my arm and pulled me up. Then he hugged me. He didn't say anything. He just placed an arm over my shoulder and hugged me until I stopped crying. The coach talked to me while the rest of team waited on the bus, explaining that he wasn't going to feel sorry for me, that he wasn't going to give me anything, and that nobody was ever going to give me anything that was worth having. He said that if I wanted playing time I was going to have to work my ass off, learn the plays, work on my fundamentals and get physically stronger. Finally, he told me he didn't know if I'd get into another game that season or not, but it was up to me to be ready in case I did.

Coach Dean and the team waited for me on the bus while I got dressed. There was no need for a shower. When I got on the bus, I waited for someone to make a crack, but it didn't happen. Finding a seat in the back, I fell asleep.

We played for third place the next day. Dean sent me into the game with the score tied in the third quarter. There was no way I was going to let the coach down. I screened off my man, grabbed a defensive rebound, kicked the ball out to Preacher and sprinted for the other end of the court. Preacher whipped the ball to Frank Louder who was at half court. I filled the right lane. Louder came to a jump stop at the free throw line and hit me with a crisp pass under the basket for a layup. Two points. The first two of my freshman year. And they were beautiful. I looked to Coach Dean.

"Keep your head in the game, Snyder!" he growled.

Logging five minutes of playing time, I racked up two points and three rebounds. We won the game, taking home the third place trophy. On the bus ride home, I sat with Preacher. When I asked him why no one gave me a hard time on the bus the day before, he said that Coach Dean had said that he would personally beat the crap out of anyone who gave me any shit, even if it meant losing his job.

Taking Barry Dean's advice to heart, I cranked out push-ups every morning, racked my brains to learn the plays, and worked hard on the fundamentals of my game. Preacher's older brother Bobby Pearl helped me develop my shot. He rebounded for me while I shot hundreds of jumpers, suggesting that I bring the ball behind my head and release more quickly in order to avoid getting swatted by older, stronger, more athletic players. And he was kind enough to seek out those older, stronger, more athletic opponents, driving Preacher, Frank Louder and me to some of the toughest gyms in Inglewood, Gardena, and South L.A. Frank Louder and I were more often than not the only white guys in the gym. Like me, Frank was a six-foot-two-inch beanpole. The brothers never ran out of unflattering nicknames for Frank and me, nicknames like the bookends, Pasty One and Pasty Two and worst of all, white boy. It wasn't long before Bobby's lessons started to take hold. After getting the ball swatted into the bleachers a few thousand times, I learned to catch the ball, quickly get it behind my head and launch my shot safely toward the basket.

By my junior year I had played varsity summer league and was a starter for the JV team. I was the second leading scorer on the team, just behind Francisco Bernard Rodriguez, the greatest athlete I have ever known. Francis set school records in basketball, football, and baseball and he went on to play wide receiver for the USC Trojans. I had some big games, but Francis Rodriguez always overshadowed me. If I scored fifteen points, he scored twenty. If I scored twenty, he scored twenty-five.

It was the last game of my JV season. We were playing against El Segundo High School. The gymnasium was packed with screaming fans. Superman Francis Rodriguez had fouled out and I had been moved from forward to high post. We were down by two with ten seconds on the clock. There were no timeouts left. Danny Martinez, who would be the best man in my first wedding, brought the ball up court slowly. Seven seconds, six seconds. I posted up on the right side of the free-throw line. Danny gave me the look. Five seconds, four seconds. Danny whipped the ball to me. Three seconds. Holding the ball hard under my chin, I could feel the defender leaning against my right shoulder. Two seconds. Lifting my right foot, I wheeled a hundred and eighty degrees on my left foot, bringing the ball behind my head. One second. Squared toward the basket, I released the ball. It felt perfect. It was perfect. The ball hit nothing but the bottom of the net as the buzzer sounded. The crowd exploded. Hundreds of my classmates went insane, jumping up and down and hugging each other. The cheering was deafening. When I realized that I had made those people lose their minds, my knees became weak and shivers ran up and down my spine. Right there in the middle of that court with the crowd cheering and teammates hugging me, I thought back to the humiliation I experienced in front of that Palos Verdes locker room just a little over two years before. We won the game in overtime. I had twenty-six points, and true to form, Francis Rodriguez had twenty-seven, but it was my night. One of my teammates Sean Duran approached me in the locker room. The two of us had never liked each other, but on this night, he offered me his hand and we shook. "Snid, you're still a dick," he said, "but you played a hell of a game." Even my enemies were giving me respect.

Stucker, the varsity coach, approached me next. "Billy, were going to do big things next year." It didn't matter if I never played another game, I had redeemed myself. I was finally the man. At least on this one night, I was the man.

My senior year didn't exactly pan out in the hoops department. Sophomore Leonard Agee was six-ten and Tracy Turner was six-six; they handled the post-positions quite nicely. In addition to Superman Francis Rodriguez, there was a glut of athletic guys to play the wings and I was no point guard. I wasn't the most consistent shooter, but I was undoubtedly the best shooter when I was hot. And I began the season on a hot streak. Over the first four games, I scored thirty points without missing a shot, in limited minutes. But Coach Stucker and I were butting heads. I wasn't happy about spending so much time on the bench.

The beginning of the end of my high school basketball career took place at the Torrance High School Holiday Tournament. Only six players, just two of them starters, showed up to play in a game against a highly ranked West Torrance team. Some were sick and others had taken Christmas trips with their families. Those of us who had showed up played above our heads. We kept the tempo slow. Since our big men Leonard and Tracy were not there, I took the post position, guarding a six-eight kid who would go on to play division one college ball. He busted my lip open with a hard elbow shot in the first quarter, but I played him tough, holding him to single digit scoring. With ten points, I was the leading scorer in a thirty to twenty-eight loss. It had taken a few games, but in my mind, I had certainly earned some serious playing time.

Coach Stucker and I had different ways of seeing things. The next game, Stucker put me in with a minute left in the first half. His instructions were clear: get the ball to big Lenny down low. Right off the bat, Preacher swung the ball to me on the wing. Lenny was calling for the ball down low, all six-ten of him. My man was sagging off of me and I was feeling it. But the coach's instructions were clear. A smart guy would have dumped the ball into Lenny; however, I was not a smart guy. I was a shooter and I was feeling it. I let go with a soft twenty-footer. It felt good. Nothing but net. Sprinting back to the defensive end, I glanced at Stucker. He looked like he wanted to put a cigar out on my face. The buzzer sounded ending the first half and I did not get back into the game.

If only I had been a smart guy.

Coach Stucker kept me on the bench the next game. That Palos Verdes lump had returned to the back of my throat. I could feel tears welling up in my eyes. I wasn't about to go back to that place. With thirty seconds left in the game, Stucker called for a time out. I made eye contact with Mike Emmanuel, the team videographer, on the other side of the court, motioning for him to turn the camera on and tape me. While the rest of the team was huddled up, I grabbed a ball from the rack and began to spin it on my index finger. I hammed it up until the buzzer went off. Motioning to Mike to wait with my free hand, I carefully switched the spinning ball from my index finger to my middle finger and then smacked the ball away with my free hand, leaving my naked middle finger pointed directly at the camera. It worked out well after practice the next day when the entire team viewed the game tape. My teammates loved it. They laughed and clapped. Stucker turned the machine off and gave me his meanest stink eye. I returned my own version of the stink eye as I walked past him and out the door. He screamed something at me, but the words were unclear. I kept walking. It was a very cool and cinematic move on my part, the kind of thing I usually only come up with when it's too late. I didn't go to practice the next day, or the next. My high school basketball career was over.

SURFER GIRL

1977

It is the summer of 1977. I am seventeen years old at the Manhattan Beach pier. The ultimate Beach Boys song radiates from a portable radio.

I have watched you on the shore
Standing by the ocean's roar
Do you love me, do you surfer girl
Surfer girl surfer girl...

Soaked with the salt water of the Pacific Ocean, I hold the battered surfboard that I purchased from Donald Bailey for five bucks. There is something disingenuous about my five dollar surfboard. The truth is I couldn't surf to save my life. The surfboard is merely a prop to make me appear more striking when I emerge from the pounding waves. It's worth noting that I am reasonably competent at the fine art of paddling. The smells of coconut flavored Coppertone suntan lotion, salt and seaweed float along the cool ocean breeze. Joe Alvarez hops along the baking sand in bare feet as he devours a square slice of Zeppy's premium, thick, cheesy pizza. The aroma is nothing short of intoxicating. Alvarez tears a bite loose, but the pizza remains connected to his mouth by a tantalizing string of perfect cheese. There is nothing quite like Zeppy's pizza. Served in square slices, the pizza is so much more substantive, at the very least, quadrupling the amount of cheese allocated by other pizza stands. Oh my God, I would do just about anything for just one bite of Joe Alvarez's square of pizza.

Ingrid Marinovich speaks and I forget about the pizza. She is stunning in her bright orange French cut bikini and her fluorescent yellow ski glasses. Her soft golden brown skin is coated with moist coconut suntan lotion. Playful beads of sweat trickle down the middle of her firm stomach and vanish tauntingly into her luscious belly button. This goddess is a member of the Hawthorne High School gymnastics team; she is well-formed, scintillatingly curvaceous. I have had a crush on this glorious creature all year. We were in German class together. I've actually been to her house – to study for a German test.

Ingrid is first generation Yugoslavian; her parents escaped to America just before the Soviet tanks rolled through the streets of their hometown. She taught me two phrases in Yugoslavian. The first is, *"Stravo. Coco si?"* It means "Hello. How are you?" The second is *"Yeti govno."* Loosely translated, it means *"Eat doo-doo."* She thinks I'm funny, laughing hysterically at even my lamest jokes. Ingrid told me she almost peed her pants when I parted my hair on the right side, placed the end of a black comb under my nose and imitated Adolf Hitler in German class. She is constantly talking about fixing me up with her friends. Of course, Ingrid doesn't understand that it's not her friends I'm interested in, that I have a crush on her. And there is no reason to tell her. She is going out with Roberto Moreno. Roberto is a bit of a local celebrity because his photograph appeared in the March issue of *Surfer Magazine*. The luckiest kid at Hawthorne High drives what is popularly referred to as *that bitchin' yellow Camaro* and smokes Marlborough Red, hard pack. I saw him in the parking lot earlier today. He was pulling out with his surfboard strapped to the top of his flawless bitchin Camaro. He acknowledged me with a "hey dude" before executing three perfectly formed smoke rings and peeling out.

Back to Ingrid. I am gawking, I mean talking to her when she offers me one of her Kools.

"Thanks, Ingrid," I say, neglecting to take into account the fact I have never smoked a cigarette.

Her hand softly brushes mine as I accept a cigarette. Her touch launches shivers down my spine, sending rhythmic reverberations through every portion of my body. A wave of dizziness overcomes me. Could it possibly be that her seemingly accidental hand brush was some kind of surreptitious indication that she prefers me over mister smoke ring blowing, Camaro driving, I'm on the cover of *Surfer Magazine* Roberto Moreno?

Ingrid fires up a Kool for herself before assisting me with the light up process. This stunning example of feminine grace takes a long seductive pull on her Kool. She absolutely sizzles as she lets out a slight moan of pleasure. Oh my God, the moan electrifies me. Could this be another signal? I take a puff before quickly exhaling. The menthol is utterly disgusting. This stinking cigarette could be the singular worst thing I have ever tasted.

"He's not even smoking," shouts some long haired punk kid leaning over the railing atop the pier.

Sheepishly, I steal a glance at Ingrid. She appears to be gazing back at me, the ends of her full lips coiled in a slight, playful smile. Could this said "gaze" be interpreted as a sign that she has wanted me all along? Oh man, does she look good in that orange bathing suit, all lathered up in cocoa butter; she's a bona fide fox, glistening in the hot California sunshine. Another exquisite bead of sweat dances tauntingly downward and into Ingrid's perfect belly button, lighting me up with good vibrations. I don't want to displease this superb Eastern Block beauty who has taught me to say "eat doo-doo" in her ancestral tongue. So I throw caution to the wind and suck in an enormous puff of menthol smoke and swallow.

Bad idea.

Within a split second the combination of menthol and tobacco shoves a throat full of vomit up to my mouth. Valiantly, I spring to the piling and unload while Ingrid and hundreds of sun tanned teenagers look on.

So I say from me to you
I will make your dreams come true
Do you love me do you surfer girl
Surfer girl my little surfer girl...

DAPHNE MORALES AND THE SILVER CORVETTE

"When my love swears that she is made of truth, I do believe her, though I know she lies…"
—Billy Shakespeare

1978

I stood in front of the bathroom mirror blow-drying my ridiculous layered crop of 1978 Keith Partridge-style hair. It's not like I was trying to grow my hair into a Keith Partridge look, but when I look at old pictures, this is who comes to mind. Once my hair was perfectly feathered back, I carefully slid into the stiffly pressed white tuxedo shirt with ruffles. Purposefully, I donned the beige slacks, the beige cummerbund, the big goofy clip-on tie, and the matching beige coat with tails. For the final touch, I laced up my white and red leather Converse All Stars. The basketball shoes were the rebellious touch. It felt good. Clean, fresh and classy. I looked good. Clearly, I believed I was the stuff that night. But it was early, real early.

In the driveway, my chariot awaited, my mother's blue and white 1968 Dodge Dart. It was – something to behold; rusted out dents from the final year of my grandfather's driving career peppered both sides. The torn upholstery was duct taped to the ceiling. Sometimes the upholstery fell loose and hung between the driver and passenger so it had to be pulled to one side in order to see each other. My grandfather stood next to the propped hood. A half-smoked Camel non-filtered cigarette dangled from his mouth. His cracked and weathered brown face expressed pride. He was prepared to hold the carburetor's butterfly flap down with a Phillips head screwdriver while I hit the gas and turned the key in the ignition; this was the only way the old Dodge would start.

My date was Daphne Morales. I had plummeted into full blown teenage love and could never imagine living without her. She had enormous, beautiful brown eyes and long black hair. Hours of training as a dancer established her strong, curvaceous figure. It's safe to say Daphne was a legitimate bombshell. We met while working together at Kinney's Shoe Store in the Hawthorne Mall. She was a cashier and I was a very bad shoe salesman. I never could latch onto the concept of trying to talk people into buying socks and other up-fronts they didn't need. Daphne Morales always wore Ditto jeans and you can believe me when I tell you the girl filled out a pair of Ditto jeans exactly the way a pair of Ditto jeans were designed to be filled out – and then some. Do you remember the scene in the old cartoons in which a hot number in a tight skirt slinks by a guy on the street corner and he jumps up, freezes in mid-air, his tongue rolls on to the ground and his eyes pop out of his head? That is precisely how I must have looked the first time I saw Daphne Morales in a pair of Ditto jeans.

The day the romance began remains crystal clear in my memory. I was in the stock room searching for a pair of size nine pumps for a lady who knew darned good and well she wore elevens. Out of nowhere, Daphne cornered me, trapped me against the shoe shelves and started kissing me. Up to this point I had been too intimidated by her to say anything more substantial than "hello." It happened just like that. Although I had just turned eighteen, I really didn't have much experience in the kissing department. Good God almighty, I can still taste the strawberry lip gloss wet on her lips! I can still feel the excitement that accompanied the possibility of being walked in on by Jim Forester, the store manager. Then I felt her soft moist lips on my neck. Holy Cow! What the hell was this? Every ounce of strength deserted my legs. I was dizzy. She was giving me what was commonly referred to as a hickey. Honest to God, I saw the fireworks and heard the *Love American Style* song.

"Hey Romeo, when you disconnect from that there suction hose, I would like to try on those nines."

It was the lady with the gun boats.

Daphne sprinted out to the cash register while I slumped to the ground with a heavenly look of stupidity on my mug.

"Yes sir, right away," I said.

Although she was a couple of years younger, Daphne ran the show. I was a basset hound and baby, she held my leash. I drove her home from work and sat through her dance classes like some kind of blithering idiot. I held her hand everywhere we went, and I wore the clothes she picked out.

The girl actually convinced me to walk around in pair of skin-tight white pants with blue stars on the back pockets. Pretty sappy, I know – and walking around in those ridiculous things gave me one of the worst rashes of my life. There was one more item. My young love didn't want me spreading it around that we were going out together. She explained that her father was from the Cuban old school and she wasn't allowed to date until she was seventeen. Daphne went to school across town at Lawndale High. Dayleen Barrientos, a pretty little surfer girl who lived on my street, told me there was a rumor that Daphne was running around with some guy at Lawndale. I blew off that warning and plenty of others. People were just jealous. Was I supposed to believe every fairy tale that went around town?

And so I rolled up in front of her house on a narrow Lawndale street. Checking my Keith Partridge hair in the rear view mirror, I straightened my silly bow tie. Leaving the car running, I got out, corsage in hand. A cool ocean breeze filled my lungs. Before I could shut the door, she was in the car, sitting on the passenger side.

"Step on it, Snyder."

I got back into the Dodge.

"Don't your parents want to take pictures?"

"If my parents wanted to take pictures, wouldn't I have asked you in to take pictures? I told you, my dad thinks you're just some loser from the shoe store who didn't have a date."

"Ouch. Why don't you just stab me in the heart, Daphne?"

"Just drive this piece of junk."

Daphne had a very dry sense of humor.

I drove her to my house where an army of family members and neighbors waited with their Kodak Instamatics poised for action. She was gorgeous in her brown dress and her golden tan with bathing suit strap lines. Back in those days, teenage girls wore their tan lines with pride. It had something to do with the contrast in colors showing the level of darkness that the skin-tanner had succeeded in achieving. I still have an old picture of the two of us standing in front of the white brick fireplace, me with a look of triumph on my face and her with a look that pretty much said, "I don't really want to be standing here with this idiot."

The prom took place at the Airport Park Marriott Hotel. There were the pictures. There were the baskets of rolls with hard little squares of butter and the chicken dinner, the ice water with lemon and all the iced tea a guy could drink. There were even a couple of slow dances with long strawberry lip gloss kisses. At some point, Daphne excused herself to powder her pretty little nose. I watched her walk away, back and forth, back and forth. It was all too hypnotic. Daphne's spell was complete. Five minutes passed. Ten minutes passed. After half an hour, I decided to wander over to the ladies restroom.

I hadn't made it three feet when my surfer buddy Danny Rich grabbed my shoulder.

"Dude, Vince Orlando is here."

"So?"

I knew Vince Orlando. He went to Lawndale and I'd played basketball against him over the years. Vince was about my height, with a wide set of shoulders and a powerful physique. Orlando was a formidable rebounder on the basketball court, but football was his real sport. He was a decent guy, always striking up a conversation when we ran into each other at summer league games and tournaments. Orlando was a rich kid and his mother was the mayor of Lawndale. Vince Orlando was best known for the 1977 silver Corvette he had received for his seventeenth birthday. More than anything else, I had always personally envied him for his ability to cultivate a thick Fu-Man-Chu since his freshman year.

"He's here for Daphne."

"That can't be true."

"Dude, they just had a big argument in the lobby. He told her she had to pick between you and him, that if she didn't come with him he was going to break up with her and start going out with Dayleen Barrientos."

"Where are they?"

"She just left with him."

This is the point in the story where everything flips into slow motion, just like in the movies. In fact, the story takes on the appearance of a foreign film.

I race for the sliding glass door. Al Green's *Let's Stay Together* is playing in the lobby. The song blasts through my psyche and rattles my soul. Danny Rich and the surfers follow in hopes that Vince Orlando and I will settle this thing with our fists.

I shout, "Daaaaaaaaphneeeeeeeee!"

My voice is distorted in slow motion too.

The silver Corvette screeches past me. I smell the burning rubber. I catch a glimpse of Vince Orlando's face. He gives me a look that says, "Sorry dude." He really is a good guy. Daphne's brown dress is caught in the passenger door of that perfect silver corvette, fluttering up and down as the car rounds the corner and is gone.

Joe Alvarez, one of the surfers, pulls up in his fluorescent orange El Camino.

"Get in, Snyder."

Joe's long blond hair hangs over the blank expression in his eyes like some kind of sun-bleached sheep dog.

"Why?" I ask.

"I'll run Vince Orlando down so you can kick his ass."

"I can't kick Vince Orlando's ass."

"You got to try, dude. He took your girlfriend. Tell you what, my skateboard's in the bed of my truck. If you get in trouble, grab my board and whack him in the face with it. It'll slow him down."

"I don't think so, Alvarez."

"We'll jump in when he starts to kill you."

"No thanks, Alvarez."

I watched a 747 pass overhead as Joe Alvarez parked his car and the surfers went back to the prom. They were disappointed. I took a deep breath. A strong Pacific Ocean breeze softened the nauseating odor of jet fuel. If I had ever felt more completely alone, I couldn't remember when. No doctor would heal this wound. Recovery would be out of the question. I would never trust another woman. Totally dejected, I headed for my mother's car. To add insult to injury, I remembered that I could not start the thing alone. I had to flag down an old couple. The couple was probably younger than I am today, but I'm digressing – again. The humiliation continued when I had to ask the guy if he would hold the butterfly flap open with my Phillips head screwdriver so I could drive myself home.

"Don't you have a date for the prom, kid?"

"Yeah Mister, but she left me for a guy with a Corvette," I said matter-of-factly.

"I don't blame her!" said the guy's wife as she stuck her face out the late model, lime green Plymouth Valiant.

We started the car and I drove to 26th Street Beach where I planned to walk along the ocean and think about how horrible everything was since this was the kind of thing that was generally done under similar circumstances in the movies. When I got to the beach, I decided to leave the engine running because I didn't want to go through the humiliation of asking someone for help and then having to explain again why I was in a tuxedo with no prom date. I put the old Dart in park and walked toward the ocean. But then I thought someone might come along and steal my mother's car. So I just kind of stood in front of the idling car for a while. It wasn't long before I started to feel like an idiot, so I got back in the car and drove home.

Clearly, my life had been irrevocably changed. My unrefined heart had been mercilessly ripped from my chest cavity in a most publicly humiliating way. The situation was not a total loss; I did get a few mercy dates. Cute girls approached me, telling me that what Daphne had done was messed up and that they would go out with me. I wasn't so leveled that I didn't take advantage of those situations. I had to do something dramatic, make a statement – that's my M.O. I would have to join the Marines or maybe the Air Force.

That would show her.

And that is how I came to be Airman Basic Snyder of 347th Training Squadron. I didn't pan out to be much of an airman. Within sixth months, I was granted a general discharge that accused me of being *unsuitable to military life*.

After being discharged, I returned to Hawthorne, hoping that Daphne Morales would come crawling back and begging to get back together. Didn't happen. We spoke from time to time, but the sizzle was gone. I would go on to have my heart broken by other pretty girls. But Daphne Morales holds a key position in my personal history because she was the first girl to level me so ruthlessly, so overtly. Furthermore, she hoodwinked me with the panache and sophistication of a latter day girl version of P.T. Barnum. Or not. Could it be that Daphne Morales was just a sixteen year-old kid with more new found attention from the opposite sex than she was capable of dealing with? Guess it doesn't matter. The point is my short and devastating teen-age romance with Daphne Morales ended with an epic explosion and when it comes down to it, in an inexplicable way, I kind of like epic explosions.

GOD'S OWN BAR

1978

Things were a little vague. I concentrated to keep the luxurious automobile on the slick mountain road. The fact that I was severely acrophobic didn't do much to help matters. The borrowed Chrysler Fifth Avenue was the finest automobile I'd ever driven, a far cry from my mother's weathered '67 Dodge Dart. The smell of the leather upholstery was nothing short of intoxicating. I had absolutely no idea where I was headed. Then again, none of us really know where we are headed now do we? You might say direction is an elaborate illusion.

My mind raced back a few hours. Sitting on the shag carpeted stairs of a trendy Boulder condominium owned by the mother of fellow airman Jim Cortes, I held a can of ice cold Coors in one hand and the banana yellow telephone receiver to my ear with the other. Taking a long pull on the Coors Light, I said, " Mom, I'm getting out."

"Slow down. You're not thinking this through."

"It's already set. The paperwork is in."

"Are they giving you a dishonorable discharge?"

"No, unsuitability to military life; it's a general discharge."

"What are you telling me, Billy?"

"I'm getting out, that's all."

"Isn't unsuitability to military life a code for homosexuality?"

"What?"

"Are you…"

"Gay? Come on. No! Heck no I'm not. Mom, how could you think that?"

"You can't do this."

"It's already done, Mom."

"I can call your recruiter."

"I don't want you to call the recruiter. I want it to be done."

She started to cry. I started to choke up myself.

"I'll call you later, Mom."

Quietly, I hung up the phone and struggled to regain my composure. Chuck Pagano and the Cortes brothers were tough kids. They kept gun racks on the back windows of their trucks and chewed Red Man. These Boulder guys were all I had. It was beginning to feel like going back to L.A. wasn't going to be an option.

A faded rust colored van with Arizona plates, a cracked windshield and more than its share of dents was pulled over to the side of the road. It was a strange model. I'd never seen anything like it. If the old bucket weren't so banged up, it might have looked a little like something out of the future. A middle-aged couple stood behind the strange van. The guy had his arm around his wife; her face was pressed against his chest. Kids were bouncing around inside the van like it was Christmas morning. It would be dark before long. By the time I considered stopping to offer a hand, they were in the rear view mirror. I breathed a sigh of relief when I watched a state trooper pull up behind the van. The couple looked mysteriously familiar. Somewhere, somehow, it felt like I'd seen them both before, but I couldn't remember where.

A few miles ahead, I pulled into a roadside gas station. The service bell rang. A lanky blonde character with sun burnt cheeks and his fists shoved into the pockets of his blue coveralls appeared at my window. I hit the button and the power window glided down. Man, what a smooth machine. It was cold out there, real cold.

"Filler 'er up, dude?"

"Better just put in ten."

I fought back the inclination to play with the electric window.

"Gnarly," he said, shoving the nozzle in the tank before taking the spray bottle to the front windshield.

Climbing out from the warmth of the Chrysler, I took a look around. The icy wind stabbed away at my cheeks. The sky was grey and just about everything else was white. The Colorado high country smelled clean and new; it smelled like starting over.

You know, you're pretty much the first guy in Colorado I've heard say gnarly or dude," I said as I watched the attendant wipe down the back window.

"I'm from Santa Monica, dude," he said, adroitly dipping a pinch of Skoal between his lip and gums. "That's ten bucks."

Opening my wallet, I pulled out a ten and handed it over. Three twenties remained. There was a freshly printed check, courtesy of United States Air Force, made out for hundred and sixteen bucks in my pocket. This was a considerable amount of walking around money in 1978.

"What are you doing up here?" I asked

"Frozen waves, bud."

"Huh?"

"Skiing, dude; righteous skiing."

I glanced over to a bar and grill. It seemed so tiny set against an endless blanket of snow capped pines.

"Is the food any good?"

"Not really," he said, "but the three-two beer's muy bueno cheap. The diner ain't gonna open for a half hour, but the bar's open."

My experience with bars had been limited to the Airman's Club on base, a few of the college bars in Boulder, and a couple of seedy strip clubs in Denver. Stepping through the front door, this place felt more – comfortable than the other joints. What's more, it was more – true. The walls were lined with elk trophy mounts. A fluorescent orange Coors beer sign flashed on and off next to the window; this was, after all, Colorado. A couple of old timers in flannel shirts were bellied up to the bar watching the highlights of a Denver Nuggets game on an old television set. The bartender was something to behold. Wearing long white hair and a flowing white beard, the old man was big, at least six-five and he had a wide set of shoulders. His skin was weathered and he wore a thick navy blue pullover sweater. I suppose he looked something like Zeus or Moses or Charlton Heston or better yet, God.

No one seemed to notice as I pulled up a stool. The television station had paused for a news break and was playing footage of the Jonestown massacre. The networks had been playing the footage for a couple of days now. It was a nightmarish scene. The lifeless bodies of men, women and children, whole families, were scattered across the Guyana compound like so much laundry that had been blown loose from the clothesline by a strong wind.

"Sheep," the bartender said, staring up at the screen.

His voice was absolutely thunderous.

"What's that?" I said

"I said sheep, son. Those people were sheep. All those people are gone, their kids too, because they didn't want to think for themselves. It was easier to let some rat bastard do their thinking for them."

Stopping for a minute, he looked right through me.

"Do you think for yourself, son?"

"I don't really know," I said.

"That could be construed as the wrong answer, my boy."

"I guess you're right."

"You know, there'll never be a more important time in your life."

"A more important time for what?"

"Beer?"

"There'll never be a more important time for beer?"

"No. Do you want a beer?"

"Oh, sorry about that. Please."

He poured a cold draft schooner and set it in front of me on the bar.

"You want to run a tab?"

"Sure."

"There'll never be a more important time to think for yourself, to figure out your own moves."

"Yeah?"

"That's right," he said. "The choices you make today, confused kid or not, are the choices you're going to live with for the rest of your life."

"That's heavy," I said.

"It is heavy," the majestic old man said as he carefully wiped the bar down with a wet rag.

Lifting the schooner, I drank half of its contents in three hard gulps. Leaning on the bar, I tried to think. My mother had to be considered. How could I disappoint her after she busted her tail for me all of those years? And then there was my grandfather. Then again, maybe not; the truth was he thought I was a dumb ass anyhow. What about Uncle Ronnie, mister hot shot Air Force colonel – wasn't he the one I had always wanted to impress? In one week I would be granted a general discharge. There wouldn't be any need to worry about what Colonel Alison thought anymore, huh? I was eighteen with a high school diploma and a hundred and seventy-six bucks to my name. What the hell was I supposed to do? I'd made a few friends in Boulder, Chuck Pagano and the Cortes brothers. Big Frank offered me a job at his burger joint. Never had much interest in the fast food business. The last few months had been lonely as hell. No family, just a revolving door of temporary friends and acquaintances. My mother would undoubtedly let me move back in and give junior college a shot. It wouldn't be too tough to line up a job at Royze Auto Parts where several of my friends were gainfully employed. But doggone it, I didn't want to go home as a failure.

The bartender placed a bowl of salted peanuts in front of me.

"You look a little confused," he said.

"It's been one those days, weeks – shoot, years, I guess."

"Hate to be the one to break it to you, but it ain't gonna get any easier either."

Looking increasingly more magnificent, the bartender walked out from around the bar and dropped a coin in the jukebox.

Pissin' in the wind
Bettin' on a losin' friend
Makin' the same mistakes
We swore we'd never make again
Pissing in the wind
And it's blowin' all over our friends
We're gonna sit and grin
And tell our grandchildren...

Jerry Jeff Walker. These Colorado people turned me on to Jerry Jeff and Skoal Bandits. Everybody in Colorado seemed to dip. I tried taking a pinch of the real stuff, placing it between my lower lip and gums, but I kept swallowing the stuff and getting sick to my stomach. Chuck Pagano, the Boulder High School Football coach's son and a formidable high school linebacker, suggested I try the Bandit pouches. The tobacco came in clean little tea bags. Pagano called them dip training wheels.

A man stood next to me at the bar.

"What can I do you for?" asked the bartender.

"Holy cow," the guy said. "Anyone ever tell you that you look like Moses, I mean Charlton Heston in *The Ten Commandments*?"

"I get that a lot."

He turned to look at me. It was the strangest thing. Quite suddenly, the time was out of joint. It felt like some kind of dream.

"Well, Moses, I'd like a beer and a shot of Jack, please."

The bartender set him up in no time.

"What brings you to this neck of the woods?"

"Family and I were driving cross country, on our way back from Michigan."

"What part of Michigan?"

"Beaver Island. You heard of it?"

"Of course I have. America's Emerald Isle, one of the most beautiful places in the world."

"You've been to Beaver Island?"

"I've been just about everywhere, friend."

"But Beaver Island? You don't get much more obscure than Beaver Island."

The barman poured himself a shot and raised his glass.

"To Beaver Island."

The man next to me raised his shot glass and I raised my schooner. We all drank. I polished off my schooner. Noticing I was on empty, the bartender turned to pour me another.

The man next to me took a slug of his beer and looked me up and down. He could have been thirty-five and he could have been fifty-five. The guy had one of those faces. He was tall, about my height, six-two or six-three, but he outweighed me by at least thirty pounds.

"How old are you?"

The man looked at me like he knew me.

"Eighteen."

He leaned in close, "What, do you have a fake I.D.?"

"In Colorado we serve three-two beer to eighteen to twenty year-olds," the bartender said as he placed the frothy schooner in front of me.

"That's kinda weird," the man said. "I thought Colorado raised the drinking age twenty years ago."

He shrugged and took a hearty swig from his beer.

"You're pretty far off the main highway, aren't you, friend?" the bartender asked.

"Yeah, we were trying to hunt down a relative of mine, a sister I never met."

"Any luck?"

"Nah. Then the fuel pump went out on the van. I knew I shouldn't have trusted that old clunker with my whole family on a cross country trip. What really pisses me off is I paid an arm and a leg for a new fuel pump less than three months ago. What the hell is that?

"That's human nature. *Caveat emptor*, baby," the bartender said, shaking his head.

"Hey," I said, "you were broken down a few miles back on the road."

"And you passed me? Thanks a lot, kid."

"The state trooper was there with you."

The man finished his beer.

"I got to check on my wife and kids next door."

He stood and headed back into the diner.

The bartender leaned in toward me.

"I take it you have a choice to make."

"How'd you know that?"

"It wasn't so tough. I guess everybody's got a choice to make at any given moment, don't they?"

"I guess so."

"So what's eating you?"

"I'm being discharged from the Air Force."

"Why's that?"

"Unsuitability to military life."

He looked over at the two old guys at the end of the bar, leaned in and quietly said, "Depending on your point of reference, that's a label that could be taken as a complement. So they're kicking you out, why?"

"I flunked my tech school tests – on purpose."

"Why?"

"Because I didn't want to be a material facilities specialist."

"What's wrong with supply?"

"Nothing, I just thought I was destined for something more. I thought I was destined for something big."

"It don't matter where you start or where you go. What matters is how you go about getting there, son. You signed a contract, put your name on the dotted line, right?"

"I guess so."

"That ought to mean something to you."

"Yeah, well, what's done is done and Uncle Sam is giving me the boot.

"What's the dilemma?"

"I don't know whether to stay here in Colorado or go back to California."

"Yeah?"

"My mother's in California. I have a place to stay in California – a home and friends. I can go to junior college."

"So what's the problem?"

"I'm embarrassed."

"Embarrassed, why?"

"Because I failed."

"And you think you're the first knucklehead to fail?"

"No, it's just that I was so confident when I left home. People warned me. Some of them said I'd be back. I don't want to face them."

"So what'll you do in Colorado?"

"I can work at a burger joint, save up for a year and go part time to college out here."

"Guess you do have a choice to make. I suppose you know what's right for you. Here's the thing, son," the big man leaned in close, "it seems like, more often than not, the toughest choice, the road you don't want to take because it's harder, is just about always the best way to go in the long run. It just about always comes down to the easy choice or the right choice."

The familiar man came back in from the diner and pulled up the stool next to me.

"The wife gave me the go ahead for one more quick beer and a shot."

The bartender poured the draft and filled two shot glasses.

"Salud," the bartender said before they tossed back their shots.

"The mechanic says he'll have us up and running in half an hour," the man turned to me. "You okay, kid?"

"Yeah," I said, "I guess I'll have it figured out by the time I'm your age."

"Hah!" the man laughed. "That's what we all think – when we're eighteen. We think there's this magic age or event that's gonna make it all okay. Well kid, that's a load of ain't the way it is."

"Amen," said the bartender.

"That's what I thought, alright," the man said. "When I turn eighteen, I'm gonna be set. When I get a good girl-friend, I'll really start living. When I graduate from college, things'll really start to sail. No wait, when I make it as a standup comic, then I'll hit the big time."

"You were a standup comic?"

"Yeah, kid. Only problem was it took me two years to figure out the jokes were supposed to be funny," he grabbed my shoulder. "That was a joke."

"Damn," I said, "I'm sorry."

"Not your fault, kid. Now you understand why I didn't make it as a standup comic. Then I thought a legitimate career as a teacher would make me happy. Then it was my own television show. Then I needed to publish my book. Lately I've been thinking I need to hunt down the sister I never met. I thought that was the missing piece. But you know what, kid? Happiness is right here," he pointed to the side of his head. "And for me it's out there in the dining room – my dazzling wife and my screwy beautiful kids. You got any family, kid?"

"Yeah, in California," I said.

"You make it right," he pointed to his ears, "up here and with those people in California."

"The man's right," said the barkeep.

He reached for his wallet.

"On the house," said the bartender. "Do me a favor and let your wife take the wheel."

"Good as done. Thanks Moses. See you, kid."

The man left his schooner nearly filled to the brim on the bar and high tailed it back into the dining room. Quite suddenly, which is so often the case when I'm drinking beer – or coffee, I realized I really had to go to the john.

I looked up to ask which direction and the bartender said, "Through the dining room and next to the kitchen doors."

I passed the glass door to the diner. The man and his wife were helping the three girls on with their coats. I felt like I wanted to connect with the family, like I already was somehow connected to the family. The guy was right, his wife really was gorgeous. I hoped to God right then and there that I would someday have a woman very much like her. And then, in an instant, I knew that I would. Didn't know why I knew, I just knew.

As I reached for the bathroom door, it swung open, and I am not making this up, Wilt Chamberlain stepped out of the john. There I was standing face-to-abdomen with Wilt Chamberlain. He was enormous of course, an honest to God giant. He had to duck through the door. Mouth agape, I was in absolute awe. Back in my eighth grade days, Wilt Chamberlain had been my idol. I wore a Wilt Chamberlain style headband everywhere I went; I even wore the thing to bed.

"Wilt Chamberlain?" I asked.

"I was when I left my house this morning."

I broke into absolute hysterics.

"Good one. Can I have your autograph?" I asked.

Immediately, I felt like a complete idiot.

"Sorry kid, I'm in a pretty big hurry. You see, I got to meet up with God."

"You mean the bartender?"

"Yeah, that's Him."

"Why do you call him God?"

"Because He's God. Why else would I call him God?"

"You mean Yahweh God? Creator of the Universe, **God**? The Father, Son and Holy Ghost God?"

"That's Him."

"You're kidding."

"No kidding."

He squeezed by me and I headed into the john.

Strange, huh? I had no idea of what to make of this: the inscrutable connection with the guy and his family, Wilt Chamberlain, and the all good, all knowing, all powerful creator of everything that exists.

Back in the bar, the bartender was putting on his sky blue down jacket. A man who looked an awful lot like Theodore Roosevelt had taken his place behind the bar.

"Wait," I said.

The bearded man turned looking completely omniscient.

"What is it, son?"

"Wilt Chamberlain is your friend?"

"You could say that."

"He said you're God."

"I am that I am."

He sounded exactly like the voice of God in *The Ten Commandments*. Theodore and Wilt shared a few hearty guffaws.

"Well, what are you doing in Colorado?"

"Are you really asking me that question?"

"I guess if you're God, you're everywhere, anywhere you want to be,"

"Anywhere I need to be."

"You're really God?"

"If you believe I'm God, I'm God."

"If it's not too much to ask, could you perform a small miracle?"

"Ever hear of faith?"

Embarrassed, I said, "Look, I'm sorry."

"Oh, okay. Just this once. What do you want me to do?"

"The pressure is too much. I can't think."

"I could send you back to before you joined the Air Force, give you a redo, but you'd miss out on a heckuva lot of experience, wouldn't you?"

"I guess you're right."

"I did give you a peep into your life thirty years from now."

"You mean the guy with the broken down van and the kids – and that gorgeous woman?"

"That's right. He's the guy who wrote your story."

"Almighty, we got to book," Wilt said, placing his gigantic hand on God's down jacket. "I got it. Why don't you smite that cockroach on the ceiling?"

The bartender looked up at the biggest cockroach I had ever seen.

"Wow. That's the biggest cockroach I've ever seen. I'm not smiting an innocent cockroach. I happen to like cockroaches."

"Really?" Wilt asked.

"That's right. Do you realize I created more than four thousand species of cockroach? How many species of people did I create, Wilt?"

"Point well taken, All Knowing," Wilt bowed his head. "How about that moose head next to the flag?"

The bartender looked at me.

"Okay," I agreed.

The great bearded man pointed his considerable finger at the moose head. The title track from *The Ten Commandments* blasted from nowhere and everywhere. Thunder rolled and lightening flashed from outside the window. A great bolt of lightning shot from His finger and smote the moose head in an instant. The two old guys at the bar cheered like the Broncos had just won the Super Bowl. Theodore Roosevelt was jumping up and down, slamming his considerable fist on the counter, and shouting, "Bully."

Wilt raised his colossal fist and said, "Right on, Almighty."

God gave me a salute and headed for the door.

"See you, Wilt," I said. "See you, Almighty…er, God."

"I'm not going anywhere, son." God said, letting the rickety door slam shut behind him.

Taking a long pull from my schooner, I stared at the remnants of the smitten moose head and set out to figure out my next move.

DAVE CRUZ

1979

It is 1979. I am nineteen again and I am spending an awful lot of time with a girl by the name of Kelly MacMurphy. Without doubt, I feel attraction toward her, but quite frankly, I am dating this girl out of vengeance more than anything else. She is a friend of Allison Bullock. Allison had the audacity to break up with me a few months ago, virtually ripping my thumping red heart from my chest cavity. Okay, maybe she didn't rip my heart from my chest cavity, but she did hurt my feelings and she definitely embarrassed me. Kelly is good looking, one of those full-figured gals. My mother does not care for this girl. She is loud and exceedingly forward, making all of the first moves in the situation. Come to think of it, I can't even begin to keep up with Kelly MacMurphy.

It is a warm summer night, Friday. Kelly and I are at the Hawthorne Community Fair with Ricardo Morales and his latest playmate. Ricardo is my roommate and he is remarkably adept at the playboy lifestyle. He is the only guy I know who actually has one of those little black books, and it's filled with scores of phone numbers. His younger sister Daphne discarded me for a guy with a silver Corvette last year, inspiring me to make a statement by joining the United States Air Force, where I spent just a few months before being discharged due to my *unsuitability to military life.*

Ricardo and I rent his oldest sister's enormous house in Hermosa Beach with six other guys, none of whom have the inclination to clean up after themselves – ever. When we go to the beach, Ricardo makes it a point to discreetly tell the girls we meet that we are young lawyers or doctors and we live in our high dollar beach house just a block away. Ricardo is always ready with a line. Once he asked a couple of sunbathing beauties to keep an eye on our metal folding chairs while we walked up to the house to make a refreshing pitcher of ice cold lemonade. They agreed. I followed Ricardo in a sprint up to the house.

"Don't worry about a thing, Billy Boy. The old lemonade trick works every time. Those girls are going to melt in our hot little hands like butter when we get back."

Making the lemonade took a little longer than it should have because we had to find the dirty pitcher and glasses and then break them away from a calcified mountain of filthy dishes in the sink. Then we had to chisel away the life forms that set up housekeeping inside the glassware.

After much hard work, we returned to our prospects on the beach. Unfortunately, a couple of mammoth body builders had taken our chairs and were talking to our girls. It was pretty tough to sound suave and sophisticated when Ricardo asked, "Hey fellas, do you think we could have our chairs back, please?"

I guess Ricardo's schemes didn't always work out.

Sorry about the digression. Now that we are back at the fair, I hear the methodic cranking of metal works and the high-pitched screams from riders on the notorious Zipper. I think I'll steer clear of the Zipper tonight. Last year, I threw up on the thing, making a mess of my date and myself. As I remember last year's little disaster, the thick aroma of corn dogs and cotton candy begins to make me feel queasy. My arm is around Kelly's perfectly rounded waist and there is something a little unsettling about this situation.

Kelly is widely known as Dave Cruz's girlfriend. People keep saying, "Hey Kelly, I thought you were going with Dave Cruz," and "Hey Snyder, isn't that Dave Cruz's girlfriend? I wouldn't want to be in your shoes when he finds out."

I do not know Dave Cruz personally. I do know his brother Richard and Ricardo Morales is a friend of Dave Cruz's. I know of Dave Cruz. Everybody knows about Dave Cruz. He is a starting defensive tackle for San Jose State and he is arguably the best street fighter in the South Bay area. Standing six and a half feet tall and weighing upwards of two hundred sixty pounds, he isn't what you would call muscular; he's just big. In contrast to his size and reputation, he bears a soft, angelic baby face. He is known and feared for his power, agility, foot speed and quick hands.

I've never actually seen Dave Cruz fight, but God knows I've heard the stories. Cruz is best known for his fight with

Kurt Moore, the toughest kid ever to come out of Hawthorne High School. Moore is six feet tall, weighs a rock solid two hundred forty pounds and is as strong as on ox. He was an all-CIF heavyweight wrestler and linebacker. Cruz and Moore are good friends but at some point they had decided that they wanted to find out who could kick whose ass. Dave Cruz knocked Moore out cold with one punch. I can only imagine what he could do to me.

Since I am not a street fighter or boxing ring fighter or any kind of fighter at all, you can surely understand why I am apprehensive to have my arm around a girl who is widely thought of to be Dave Cruz's girlfriend. I ask Kelly, for the hundredth time, if she is sure that Dave Cruz doesn't mind us going out.

"It's cool, Bill," she says. "Besides he's in San Jose this weekend."

"But you guys are broke up, right?"

"Well, he messes around with other girls."

This doesn't sound right.

"But you're broke up, right?"

"It's an unspoken thing, Bill."

I am thinking about the unspeakable things Dave Cruz might do to my face.

No, this doesn't sound right at all, but Kelly sends me this seductive come hither look, squishes her curvaceous body in close to me and gives me a long wet kiss. I become stupid and do not care about Dave Cruz. Kelly MacMurphy is pretty hot. Her moist tongue fills my ear, right in front of God and the cotton candy man and everyone. I begin to melt. Shivers are skittering up and down my neck. I am lightheaded. There is the blazing passion, the obnoxious carnival barkers, the smell of cotton candy, the screaming from the Zipper, and Dave Cruz.

Dave Cruz?

"Isn't that Dave Cruz?" I hear Ricardo say.

It is Dave Cruz. He has just rounded the corner of the milk bottle game booth accompanied by fellow tough guys Kurt Moore and Keith Jones. Dave Cruz is standing maybe fifteen feet away. Stuffed pink flamingos hang next to his enormous head. Just like in the cartoons, he gives me an exaggerated double take. He looks somewhat upset. His sun burnt baby face looks dangerous. I feel what my cave man ancestors must have felt when they came face to face with raging bears. Adrenaline fills my body. The fight-or-flight instinct takes control and I ain't about to fight. Sure, I fear the pain, but more than that, I fear the humiliation of being beaten senseless in front of all of these people.

Dave Cruz's eyes lock in on mine. He sneers. At this point, Dave has been standing across from me for perhaps a second. I lean to Kelly's ear and say, "I got to go to the bathroom." This is not a lie. It is nothing short of a miracle that I have not already wet my pants. Instantly, I let go of my newly purchased cup of Pepsi, pivot and run. Before Kelly can reply, I run like nobody's business. Before my Pepsi cup hits the asphalt, I run like I've never run before. Now I'm not the most athletic guy in town. I get by on the basketball court with my decent jump shot and solid understanding of the game, not my quickness or agility. But tonight I move with sleek grace and perfection. And I look good as I run from Dave Cruz. The lights from the rides and the game booths turn to Star Wars-like hyperspace streaks. I leap over baby strollers and dodge balloon salesmen with great ease. Bobby Agee, the star running back of Hawthorne High's football team, has nothing on me. Not tonight. Tonight, I am *The Juice*. I do not look back because I know how fast Dave Cruz is and I understand that looking back can cost time. I come to an eight-foot chain link fence with three strands of razor sharp barbed wire at the top. I do not stop. I do not think. I hope somebody is watching as I execute the most athletic move of my life, grabbing the chain link fence with my left hand, my momentum propels me to flip gracefully over the barbed wire, feeling like Bruce Lee as I drop with catlike grace on the other side.

"Please God, make sure that somebody saw that move," I say to myself. But I do not stop or look back. Dave Cruz is fast and capable of exploding right through that chain link fence. I sprint the three blocks to my mother's house in what I am sure is Olympic record time. With Dave Cruz on my tail, I am the fastest man in the world. I rocket through the tree lined neighborhood of my formative years. Danny Rich's mother is watering her lawn and she speaks to me as I pass. Einstein's physics have come into play. I am moving too fast to make out the words and she looks warped and distorted from the corner of my eye. Easily, I vault the hedges alongside my mother's house. Three smooth strides bring me down the driveway to the swinging gate to the back yard. Effortlessly, I hurdle the gate and crouch behind to watch for Dave Cruz. My breathing is hard and irregular. I am soaked with sweat. My heart rages inside.

But Dave Cruz does not come. Maybe I lost him. Perhaps he never came after me. It could be that the notion of shooing me away like some pesky housefly has satisfied him.

"What the hell are you doing, you lug head?"

It is my grandfather.

"I'm hiding from Dave Cruz."

"What?"

"Yeah, I was at the fair with his girlfriend and I was afraid he was gonna kick my ass so I ran."

"You ran? I never ran from anyone in my life."

"Yeah grandpa, but I looked good."

STANLEY GOLDEN

1982

One of the most coveted college jobs in Los Angeles had to be that of an usher at the fabulous Forum and I was lucky enough to have one of those jobs. The Laker games were the hottest tickets in town. Celebrities were everywhere. On any given night, I interacted with the likes of Chevy Chase, Gene Hackman, Sly Stallone, Arnold Schwarzenegger, and Paul Simon. One night, Bo Svenson took it upon himself to shove me to the ground when I asked to see his ticket. How many guys can say that? Everyone wanted to see the Showtime Lakers with Magic Johnson, Kareem Abdul Jabbar and my old high school nemesis Byron Scott.

It was halftime. Paula Abdul and the Laker Girls were doing their thing at mid court. By the way, Paula Abdul had a crush on me in those days. She always made it a point to walk by me and bat her eyes. I'm pretty sure I could have had her – really. I'm not kidding. She once walked past me, read my name tag and said, "Hello Buzz." Buzz, that's the nickname I picked up working at the Forum. Yeah, working at the Forum was cool, very cool.

The trumpets and tubas of the USC marching band were absolutely rocking the building. I had been assigned to stop patrons from moving past me until Brent Musburger had finished his television interview. Most people were cooperative when I asked them to wait. I was basking in the energy of the crowd as the Laker Girls did their thing at center court when an obnoxious New Yorker shoved his way through the wall of humanity. He was short and stocky, dressed like one of the jokers in the movie *Saturday Night Fever*. The guy was sporting lots of gold chains and a Rolex. If it weren't 1982, he would have been talking loudly into a cell phone. I stepped in front of him.

"I'm sorry sir, but you'll have to wait until the interview is over."

"Who are you supposed to be?"

I hated guys like this.

"I'm just asking you to hang in there until the interview is over."

"I don't think you know who I am," he said as he attempted to barrel past me.

Standing my ground, I took on my best aggressive demeanor. Although I was no tough guy, I had become adept at acting like one. I had thrown my share of drunks out of concerts and broken up plenty of fights. And there was always help a few seconds away.

"I don't care who you are, and you're not goin' past until the interview's over," raising my voice considerably, I said, "Now get back!"

The guy was furious.

"I'm Stanley Golden and here's my ticket!"

He shoved the ticket in to my face.

"Get back!" I was getting loud.

Francis Rodriguez was backing me up.

Stanley shoved the ticket closer to my face.

"Look at my ticket, dammit!"

I shouldn't have taken the ticket. I don't know why I took the ticket, but I did and held it close to my eyes in order to examine it.

SMACK!

My head rocked backward and the salty taste of blood filled my mouth. A loud buzzing filled my head. The son of a bitch had cold cocked me.

Francis Rodriguez, who was six-three and solid as a rock, scooped up my assailant. I grabbed hold too. We carried him like a surfboard. The idiot was cursing and screaming.

"You can't throw me out!"

We were moving through the crowd toward the exit tunnel. Pumped up with anger and adrenaline, I was about to start yelling back when I heard someone laughing in the crowd. At first I was insulted. Some joker was laughing at me because I got slugged in the mouth. But the laughter sounded familiar. Francis and I both stopped and looked at the laughing man. Dressed in a fishing hat and his trademark black shades, it was Jack Nicholson.

"Nice goin' boys. Now take him out back and kick his ass. I saw the whole thing. The little son of a bitch deserves it! Ha, ha, ha."

We moved past Nicholson and into the tunnel. The New Yorker's cursing and screaming was echoing in the empty concrete hallway. Glancing over my shoulder, I could still hear Nicholson at the end of the tunnel.

"Kick that son of a bitch's ass back there! Ha, ha, ha."

We rounded the corner for the North Hole, a secret exit used for the purpose of tossing out drunks and idiots. Eric Steinman, a law student and the permanent guardian of the North Hole, put his book down and opened one of the two large metal doors. Francis guided Stanley Golden's head into the bar of the other metal door – the closed one, forcing it open.

"OOOOW! You can't do that! I'm Stanley Golden."

We gave the guy the heave ho and sent him sprawling over the wall and into the bushes. Blood was now trickling down my chin and onto my gold toga. The guy stood up in the ivy and held out his ticket.

"You can't throw me out, I got a ticket."

Francis hopped the fence, walked down to him, snatched the ticket from his hand and said, "Good night, Stanley." Francis ripped the ticket into tiny pieces and tossed them up in the air. The pieces fluttered to the ground as Francis climbed back over the wall and we stepped back into the building. Eric pulled the door shut hard and loud.

"I'll sue you both! WHITE TRASH!"

His voice was muffled on the other side of the doors.

Chalk one up for white trash.

Eric went back to his studies and Francis and I returned to the floor. When we walked past Nicholson he lifted his eyebrows high above his shades and shot us a slick smile. He tilted his head to read my name tag and said, "Nice goin' – Buzzz."

The world is full of Stanley Goldens. And sometimes it seems like they get all of the breaks. So when the Stanley Goldens of the world get me down – and they do get me down – a lot, I think back to Jack. I see him standing there laughing and I hear him saying, "Take him outside and kick his ass. Son of a bitch deserves it." And I remember that every once in a while the Stanley Goldens of the world get just exactly what they deserve.

HANK

1984

I showed up at Steve's house as usual at seven. Steve let me in. Making a beeline to the pot, I poured myself a cup of coffee that had the consistency of 10-40 weight motor oil, and had a seat on the old green couch in the living room. The coffee was good. Coffee is always good in the morning. The walls were covered with surfing posters and Frisbees. Steve sat at the kitchen table where he carefully went about the business of lacing up his work boots.

Steve Vanderwall was a big guy, six-foot-five, maybe two hundred forty pounds. He was a prototypical California surfer. Bearing curly blonde locks, blue eyes, and beet red skin, he used words like *dude, bitchin* and *gnarly* a lot. I think I even heard him say *cowabunga* once. Big Steve had a part time gig with Whammo as a professional Frisbee trick guy. Girls really dug him. As a matter of fact, he had chumped me a couple of years earlier in Palm Springs. My girlfriend (at least I thought she was my girlfriend) Allison was spending the Memorial Day weekend in the desert town with a few girlfriends. I came up with the brilliant idea of showing up to surprise her.

When I found Allison, she was hugging Big Steve. Apparently, he thought it was pretty funny when I shouted, "Aha!" and demanded that he take his hands off the shoulders of my girlfriend.

"You kill me, dude."

That was all he said before he turned and walked off with my girl, laughing all the way. He was lucky I didn't put a beating on him right then and there. I might have done it too – if I had known karate and had access to a Louisville Slugger.

All was forgotten. At this point, he was dating my sister. As for myself, I had hit rock bottom. Although I had just learned my mother was in the process of dying of cancer, I really hadn't latched onto the reality of the situation. Instead, I seemed to be focusing on the fact that my latest girlfriend had broken up with me. Either there were some complicated coping mechanisms at work within my mind or I was unforgivably selfish. After graduating from college with a degree in radio, TV and film communications, I couldn't seem to find work in my field. Even the most menial jobs as a page or mail room clerk seemed to be out of my reach. Working as Steve's landscaping laborer was one of a long string of low paying jobs I had held since finishing college.

Once his boots were secured, Steve walked over to the coffee pot, filled a forty ounce mug, and drained the hot coffee in a matter of seconds. His red face became redder. Shaking his head like a wet dog, he made a grunting noise. He performed the hot coffee chugging trick every morning. I considered the coffee trick one of the perks of the landscaping business. We squeezed into Steve's dented black mini truck and headed out to Arnold's place in Manhattan Beach. Arnold was the boss. Just thirty years-old, he had built a thriving landscaping business, serving the beach cities and the Palos Verdes Peninsula. Arnold gave Steve the instructions for the day while I drank more coffee.

"Put in a dozen color flats at the Rambis place over at Manhattan Village and then knock out Hank's yard."

"It's been five, maybe six months since we did any maintenance at Hank's, so the shrubs should be pretty gnarly," Steve said.

"You know you love going out to Hank's because he gives you free beer," Arnold laughed.

"I ain't gonna lie to you, Arnie."

We loaded the color flats and a few maintenance tools onto the white Pacific Coast Landscaping truck and headed out to the Rambis place. I had been looking forward to this job. Kurt Rambis was a power forward for the Los Angeles Lakers. He was a tenacious rebounder and defender, a role player, but his function was quite vital. People labeled him an over-achiever because he was white. Great black players are called physically gifted and great white players are considered overachievers. While Kurt Rambis did play with tremendous heart, he was gifted with incredibly quick hands and he was one of the strongest guys in the league. Rambis had an unusual look, wearing thick Clark Kent style glasses, shaggy hair and a thick mustache. We planted the flowers within a half an hour and were back on the road. Rambis didn't so much as peek out the window.

"Where's Hank's house?" I asked.

"San Pedro. You know, old Hank is pretty famous," Steve said.

"Really? What for?"

"He's a writer."

"What's his last name?"

"His name is Charles Bukowski. Hank's a nickname. It's what he calls himself in his books."

"Never heard of him."

"Yeah, he walks down the street for beer and tacos in Pedro and no one bothers him. But I guess they mob him on the streets in Europe. He's like a rock star over there."

"Really? Why? I mean how come he's famous there and not here?"

"Beats me. You're the college boy."

"What kind of stuff does he write?"

"You know me dude. I don't read books, but Arnie's read some of his stuff. He said Hank's books are pretty crazy. I guess this joker writes about getting drunk, getting his ass kicked, betting on horses and getting laid. One book's about when he was a mailman and he had all these babes on the route. Arnie said it's pretty funny. He wrote another book called *Women.* It's a book about all of the women he screwed."

I was intrigued.

San Pedro is located on the Palos Verde's Peninsula. The town occupies a steep hill, dropping off into the L.A. Harbor.

The Vincent Thomas Bridge connects San Pedro to Long Beach. I've always felt drawn to that bridge. The combination of size and grace moved me. When I had a few extra minutes, I went out of my way to cross the Vincent Thomas Bridge on my way to Long Beach State, even if I did have to pay a fifty-cent toll. I had a few friends in San Pedro. It was a working class town that seemed better suited for the East Coast than L.A. It seemed that firefighters or longshoremen led all of the households. Everybody I knew from San Pedro fit into these three ethnic/religious groups: Italian-Catholic, Yugoslavian-Catholic, or Mexican-Catholic.

We pulled off Gaffey and onto 1st Street and rolled past Leo's Bar. Leo's was known as a black bar and there were stories of unsuspecting white guys who had ventured in and been beaten to within inches of their lives. I always wanted to walk into Leo's just to prove those stories were hogwash. I liked going into blue-collar bars. My mind drifted to the Hop Inn, just a few blocks from my house in Hawthorne. Most of the customers were Northrop Aircraft assembly line guys. I used to stop in with a few ushers after the Lakers and Kings games for a beer. We shot pool with the blue-collar guys and they seemed to get a kick out of mixing it up with a bunch of snot-nosed college kids. The Hop Inn had recently been crossed off of my list of drinking establishments. I take no pride in my reason for staying away. A couple of weeks earlier, I was at the Hop Inn, feeling desperate and angry. I was three sheets to the wind. Unsteadily, I walked out to the parking lot with a dozen or so fellow ushers, and made my way to my battered white Volkswagen Bug. Inside, I started the car and threw the stick shift into reverse, promptly crashing into the bar owner's brand new Porsche Carrera. In the rear-view mirror, I watched Pat Rodriguez, Tony Frink and Danny Martinez gesticulating wildly and screaming at me to stop. But I was having none of it. I sped out of the parking lot and onto the empty streets, checking for headlights behind me. There weren't any. It was a clean break.

"This is it, Billy boy," Steve said.

He drove the massive white truck up the long driveway to Charles Bukowski's Spanish style bungalow. The place was a wreck. The yard looked like a jungle with all of its overgrown shrubs and trees. The lawn was at least three feet high.

"Watch out for two-by-fours with nails," I said.

"What?" Steve asked.

"Nothin'."

"This is a maintenance job, Bill. We'll sweep right on through and clean everything up and make it look real bitchin. Shouldn't take us more than a couple hours. We'll work an hour, and then break for lunch. Arnie's springing for tacos from Elmer's."

I selected a large pair of shears and attacked the shrubs as if my life depended on it. Hard work was a reliable escape. Steve was still unloading the truck and I had just broken into a sweat when I saw Charles Bukowski for the first and last time. He emerged from the front door looking like a street corner wino. This was it? The great writer? Bukowski was in his 60s at the time. He wore his thick gray hair slicked back and much longer than I was used to seeing on old men. His beard was ratty, and there were a dozen or more wart-like bubbles growing on his nose and cheeks. The old guy was wearing the clothes of a workingman. In fact, he was dressed very much like my grandfather, with a flannel shirt, grey trousers, and black shoes, undoubtedly steel toed.

"Hey, Hank. How's it goin'?" Steve shouted.

"Hey, Steve-baby. Good to see you!"

"Goin' to the track, Hank?"

"Every day, baby. Every day."

"Ain't this a little early for you Hank?"

"I want to get out of here before those Hollywood pussies call."

"Okay, Hank. We'll be done in a couple of hours."

"You know there's beer in the fridge, baby. Who's the kid?"

"This's Bill, Hank."

Charles Bukowski nodded to me and I nodded back. He looked mean, like he was thinking about slugging me. The illustrious writer turned away, climbed into his little Volkswagen bug and rocketed down the hill to 1st Street.

I busted my tail cleaning up Bukowski's yard. There were thorns, lots of thorns. My arms were scratched up and bleeding. I took solace in the pain, itching, and sneezing. My hay fever was in full swing when we broke for lunch.

"Let's grab some beers, Billy," Steve said.

In the garage was an old white fridge, fully stocked with ice cold Coronas. Steve grabbed three and I did the same. I followed Steve into the house. The floors were hardwood and there were cats, perhaps a half-dozen of them. I was never much of a cat man. They cause me to sneeze and my eyes to itch. There were several black and white photographs of Bukowski. His girlfriend Linda was a photographer and

Bukowski must have been her favorite subject. There was a desk with an old typewriter. Stacks of freshly typed poems were piled next to an empty wine bottle.

"Yeah, Hank types and drinks wine all night. Then he sleeps till noon before he heads out to Hollywood Park for the afternoon races," Steve explained.

"Who are the Hollywood pussies he was talking about?" I asked.

"I guess they're making a movie out of one of his books. And Sean Penn and Mickey Rourke are always following him around. But old Hank, he can't stand 'em. He calls 'em paper tigers."

The kitchen counters were lined with hundreds of bottles of vitamins. There was a recipe for a hangover remedy on the refrigerator door. We sat at the kitchen table and began working on our tacos and cervezas.

"I guess the guy likes his Corona," I said.

"Nope, he put these in the fridge for us. Linda only lets him drink red wine. She's really into health and nutrition. Hank used to be a hard-core beer and whiskey drinker, now he sticks with the red wine and Linda makes him take her healthy vitamin concoctions. He says he'd be dead if it weren't for Linda."

The tacos were good and the beers were cold. I was glad to get back outside because the cats had really gotten my allergies operating. We knocked out the job with time to spare. There was satisfaction to be had from planting and pruning, from carrying out the job and knowing that I earned my pay. The sweat felt good as it ran down my face and the back of my shirt and burned the scratches on my forearms, diverting my mind from the things I didn't want to think about. It felt good to be dirty.

We loaded up the tools and the huge mound of green trimmings onto the truck. On the way back to Manhattan Beach, Steve told me that Arnold had witnessed Bukowski spit in a reporter's face at a party.

Looking back at that dark period in my life, I realize that the Bukowski sighting fit the tone. Over the next ten years, I would read everything Bukowski wrote, the poems, the short stories, and the novels. Charles Bukowski is gone now. He lived a hell of a long time, considering the extra wear and tear, the fights, the cheap booze, the horses, and all of those women. Charles Bukowski never conformed and I respect that. He wrote about everything in his life. No topic was left untouched. There was a time, back when life was so much less meaningful, when I felt a strong connection to his writing. Now that I have children and a wife and a home and a place in the world, Hank's grey world just doesn't seem to apply.

THE WORST WATERMAN IN THE WORLD

1986

There is a distinct possibility that I was the worst waterman ever to wear the Sparkletts uniform. Two and a half years out of college, I had experienced short careers as a bad insurance claims adjuster, a fairly satisfied landscaper's assistant, a standup comedian, a cable television host, and a waiter. I also had forked over three hundred bucks in order to earn a certificate from the American School of Bartending. Believing I was headed nowhere, I decided it was time to take on a real job. A friend was pulling in a good income with a Sparkletts Water route. He put a word in for me and I was promptly hired. My official starting position was that of a relief waterman. It was my responsibility to cover the established water guys' routes when they called in sick or went on vacation. Sometimes the route directions were good and sometimes they weren't so good. I rapidly established myself as a terrible relief waterman, constantly getting lost and often coming in from my routes long after the sun went down. While I certainly hated the job, I did undergo some valuable experiences. Delivering water allowed me to see how a true cross section of Los Angelinos lived. I saw the insides of thousands of homes over my six months with Sparkletts. I delivered water to the wealthiest neighborhoods and the poorest neighborhoods, as well as some of the toughest parts of town.

The scariest place I delivered water was a massive cul-de-sac of apartment complexes, probably a half-mile long, located in south Los Angeles, known as *The Jungle*. The regular water guy was a former NBA basketball player by the name of Randy Smith. I was assigned to his route the week he vacationed in Spain. It's a little strange to imagine a guy delivering water in *The Jungle* one week and sipping sangria on a Spanish beach the next. It might be considered strange to imagine a guy making the transition from professional athlete to waterman, couldn't it? But I guess life is like that. You might think delivering water would be an enormous financial step down for a former professional athlete, but some water guys were pulling in six figures. And this was the mid-eighties. This particular former pro had played into the late seventies when NBA salaries were nowhere near the infinitesimal amounts that have become commonplace today. Randy gave me perfect instructions for the route. He had been robbed at gunpoint while working his route more than once. The man talked about being robbed matter-of-factly. I didn't get the idea he felt anger or fear over the situation. To Randy, the experience of staring down the barrel of a loaded gun and the probability that it would happen again were just part of the territory. It was one of the best paying routes in L.A. and he was willing to take a little yin with his yang. Or is it yang with his yin?

"Bill, you got to be part of the streets. You got to blend in. Don't ask no questions. You don't want nobody thinking you scared. They'll eat you up if they do, Bill. An' make sure you keep a twenty with you all the time, cause if somebody wanna rob you, you better have somethin' for 'em."

The Bloods street gang controlled this neighborhood. A couple of pumped up, ferocious looking dudes in red sat on the hoods of late model sedans on either side of the street at the entrance to *The Jungle*. The same two guys were there every day. Making it a point not to look directly at them, I just drove right by, giving it my best to be part of the scenery. Following Randy's advice to the letter, I kept that crisp twenty dollar bill in my pocket, ready to give it up at any time. When obvious gang members approached I was fully prepared to reach into my pocket and pull out that twenty. I kept waiting for someone to stick a gun in my face, but it never happened. The boys in red never said boo to me. With Randy's precise directions, there were no surprises. My week in *The Jungle* ran snag free. As a matter of fact, it was the only route I finished on time every day. Go figure.

I delivered a lot of water to poor undocumented Mexican immigrants. These folks from Mexico didn't trust the same L.A. tap water I drank every day of my life. Most of the homes were neat and clean inside. Dinnertime deliveries were especially tough because the food smelled so darned good. I can still savor the mouthwatering aroma of frijoles and tamales being prepared in those tiny kitchens. I was usually far behind schedule and wouldn't be eating until much later. I'm telling you it was murder. Another thing worth mentioning is that these poor Mexicans who worked for less than minimum wage always paid their water bills on time. More than once, I came upon vacant apartments with little white envelopes with a few bills tucked inside addressed to *aguacero* (water man). The people had gone back to Mexico without a trace but made it a point to pay what they owed. I guess to them, it was about honor.

Delivering in the Santa Monica Hills was the worst. I was a terrible truck driver and I've always been scared to death of heights. One particular driveway still gives me chilling nightmares. The narrow asphalt road twisted and turned almost a mile up the side of a steep mountain overlooking the Pacific Ocean. Driving up that mountain, I was absolutely overcome with fear. Although I hugged the mountainside, there couldn't have been more than a couple of feet between the wheels of the truck and that jagged cliff. Driving with the greatest of care, it took me fifteen minutes to ascend that wicked hill. The route instructions called for turning around at the circular driveway in front of the stately manor at the top. Imagine my horror when I saw that the circular driveway was under construction and completely blocked off. I would have to back that lime green monster down that unforgiving road that jutted down hundreds of feet to the treacherous rocks and the hungry sea below.

"Wait a minute," I thought. "I don't have to back that big ass truck down this mountain. I could throw the keys off of this cliff and into the ocean. I could walk down this mountain to Pacific Coast Highway and hitchhike home. Someone would pick me up, maybe a beautiful surfer girl. Yeah, I could tell her my story and she'd feel bad about all of the trouble I've been through and…"

That's what I thought about doing. It's not what I did. Perhaps it would have made for a better story, but I chose to back that cumbersome green truck down that mile stretch of road three feet at a time. I backed up a yard or so, and then got out to see where the hell I was. Then I did it again, and again, and again. I must have repeated this process five hundred times. It took me almost two hours to get halfway down that hill. By that time my hamstrings were killing me from climbing in and out of the cab. I might have given up and walked down that mountain if the construction workers hadn't finished and wanted to get home to their families. Halfway down that road, they were cursing at me and telling me to hurry up. My head felt like it was going to explode. My ticker was beating hard. It felt as if I could have looked down at my Sparkletts shirt and seen my heart leaping in and out of my ribcage. I was ready to go insane. Those construction guys just kept on screaming at me.

"Come on you jackass, move that goddamned truck."

"Vamanos, you stupid pendejo!"

They were letting me have it in two languages. It got to the point where I couldn't take it any more. Slamming down on the parking brake, I leapt from the cab. Standing in front of that ugly green truck with my fists balled up, I was ready to fight every one of those sons of bitches.

"IF ONE OF YOU DUMB BASTARDS WANTS TO BACK THIS GODDAMNED THING DOWN, BE MY

GUEST! OTHERWISE, SHUT THE HELL UP WHILE I DO THE BEST I CAN! Dammit."

The boss turned to a little Mexican guy with a graying moustache and a Magic Johnson basketball jersey.

"Pedro, back the truck down for this kid, will ya?"

Pedro sprinted past me and into the cab.

"Get in, *keed*," he said to me with a smile as big as Fresno, California.

I got in on the passenger side and Pedro threw the gearshift into reverse and backed that truck down the hill going thirty or forty miles an hour. He was talking about Pat Riley, Jack Nicholson, the benefits of the Lakers' Showtime offense and I don't know what the hell else. He kept diverting his eyes from the road to look at me. It's a wonder I didn't pass out. At the bottom he stuck the gearshift into park, hopped out and said, "Go do your job, *keed*."

I guess the *keed* owed Pedro one.

For some inscrutable reason, the day I delivered water to Randy Newman remains clear in my mind. Newman was riding the fame of his hit song *I Love L.A.* Following the instructions in the route book, I knocked on the massive front door. The door opened and there he was standing right in front of me. He was wearing boxer shorts and no shirt. His white hairy gut lopped over his polka dot boxers. The little guy was squinting without his glasses and his bushy head of hair was all over the place. I got the idea Randy Newman just might have been a little hung over. I'll never forget what he said to me that day. "Put the water by the piano." Just like that. "Put the water by the piano."

There were lots of waterman brushes with fame. *Lost in Space* was one of my favorite shows when I was a kid so I lit up like a Christmas tree when I saw June Lockhart's name in the route book. She answered the front door and showed me where to put the water. Naturally, June Lockhart was much older than the sexy *Lost in Space* June Lockhart in that skintight silver space suit I had in mind. This June Lockhart was dressed in a worn plaid bathrobe. Perhaps she was having a bad day, but this June Lockhart appeared to be a cat lady. Man, cats were everywhere. They were rubbing against my legs. Did I mention that I am allergic to cats? Did I mention that I hate cats? Quite frankly, I wanted to kick just one of them, to send just one of those feline pests across the room and skidding across the expensive marble floors, but June stayed near by. Don't get me wrong, I've never kicked a cat. I'm not that kind of person. Then again, you never know, I might have kicked one of June Lockhart's – given the opportunity. The house smelled of kitty litter boxes and I could see cat hairs floating whimsically across the rays of golden sunlight that were shooting through the massive custom windows. June Lockhart needed eight bottles of water. By the time I finished dropping off the eight bottles I was sneezing and my eyes were nearly swollen shut, itching nearly to the point of insanity. Outside of the Lockhart house, I sneezed as I was backing up, causing me to slam the truck into a red brick wall. This was just one of my several minor driving accidents while delivering Sparkletts water. No, I can't say I enjoyed delivering water to June Lockhart. Very disappointing.

There were other celebrity encounters, including O.J., Linda Rondstadt, Olivia Newton John, Lionel Ritchie, Aaron Spelling, Arnold Schwarzenegger and Maria Shriver, and Lorne Greene. It was just part of the job. I did get a kick out of Lorne Greene's dogs. They were a real scroungy looking pack. Lorne Greene hosted an endless stream of television dog food commercials with the dogs. He was always talking about how his dogs were something like eight hundred years old in dog years. I felt this TV respect for Lorne "Ben Cartwright" Greene. I'm not really a dog guy, but I took a break at Lorne Greene's house, sitting on the running boards of the truck to spend a few minutes with his loveable horde of ugly mutts. It gave me a feeling of being somehow connected with the Ponderosa, Pa, Little Joe, Hoss, and Hop Sing. But not Adam. Never cared much for Adam, just couldn't feel any connection with Adam. I suppose he was a little too white-collar for my liking.

My most powerful Sparkletts delivery encounter was with James Arness. *Gunsmoke* was a significant component of my childhood. Channel surfing past the show brings back warm memories of Saturday nights at my grandparents' house. I can recall emerging from the bathroom, scrubbed down and smelling of fresh talcum powder. There was the sound of the *Gunsmoke* theme song and the smell of buttered popcorn and there were usually root beer floats involved. Oh yeah, those are good memories. My favorite *Gunsmoke* character was Marshal Dillon's deputy Festus with his countrified wisdom. I loved to watch Festus take Doc down a notch or two. I've got a cousin who talks just like Festus.

The route book instructions called for dropping the bottles off at the back door. I was disappointed; I'd been hoping to meet the big man. I knew a lot of trivia about James Arness. I knew his brother was Peter Graves, the tall towheaded guy from *Mission Impossible*. I also knew that James Arness had served in combat during World War II. He was with Macarthur when the general fulfilled his promise to the people of the Philippines and did return. Somebody ordered Big Jim to get out of the boat before McArthur to test the depth of the water because he was six-seven. One of his first show business gigs was playing the part of the monster in *The Thing*. He had also made an exceptionally cool movie called *Them*. It was about this apocalyptic invasion of giant mutant ants. My favorite line came toward the end when this stereotypical little professor with big glasses discovered the weakness of the giant insects and said in his robotic scientist's voice, "The antennae, shoot for the antennae, they are helpless without them!"

Following the directions, I carried two bottles up the driveway, one over my shoulder, and gripping the other with my arm extended straight up and down. I was surprised that James Arness lived in a normal house. Nothing ostentatious. No security guard. No swimming pool. In fact, the place wasn't much different than the house in which I grew up. It couldn't have been bigger than two thousand square feet, with a driveway on the side of the house leading to a garage in the backyard. The backyard fence was chain link. I wondered if he'd been through some kind of divorce. Maybe he was just frugal. As I made my way through the open chain link fence into the back yard, I heard a deep voice.

"You're doing it wrong, son."

I looked up the steps to the back door and there he was, bigger than life. Most of the movie stars I had occasion to run across were much smaller than they looked on screen. Sylvester Stallone, Eddie Murphy, Carl Weathers, Dorian Hayward and Andrew Stephens from *The Bastard* come to mind. They were little guys. James Arness did not fit this mold. He was an old school cowboy actor. He had appeared with John Wayne in his movies. The Duke liked to surround himself with men who where even bigger than he was, guys like Ward Bond, Victor McLaughlin, Harry Carry and James Arness. The man had to duck to look out the back door. Although he was in his sixties, he was in great shape, looking like he still hit the weights everyday. He was wearing a clean white undershirt, a faded pair of Levis and pair of moccasins.

"Huh?" I grunted.

Seeing Marshal Dillon taking up that entire doorway stirred something up inside me. I suppose I was in awe.

"You're carrying those bottles wrong. You're going to end up with back trouble. Take it from me, you don't want back trouble. You should take one bottle at a time, over your shoulder, even if it takes you longer."

He knew what he was talking about. I had been trained to carry the bottles one at a time and over the shoulder.

"I know, you're right, but I'm so far behind schedule."

I lifted the bottles up to Marshal Dillon with a grunt. He took them from me, handling them like they were one gallon instead of five. The man cut an imposing presence. The sun was in his face. He looked at me for a second, squinting against the bright rays. I'd seen that squint a hundred times on *Gunsmoke*. Damn, I wished I could squint like that.

"You look like hell. You want a soda?"

Sweat was pouring down my face and back, my shirt was untucked and I was a nervous wreck from trying to do this job for which I had no aptitude.

"Thanks," I said.

James Arness turned and walked into the kitchen. I wiped the stinging sweat from my eyes and removed my sweat-soaked cap. He filled the door and tossed me a can of Coke.

"Thanks, Mr. Arness."

He looked so smooth standing in that doorway, just like he did as Marshal Dillon. This man was really something, a real doorway-filling American cowboy star. Not one of these half-pint modern stars. James Arness was a real man. He had put himself in the line of fire during World War II, unlike chicken hawks like John Wayne and Ronald Reagan. I couldn't respect the Duke and the Gipper, not as men. These guys didn't risk their lives in time of war; they used their position and connections to get out of serving in World War II, yet it seemed like they were always popping off, questioning those who avoided the draft or spoke out against the war in Vietnam.

Tucking the ice cold Coke under my arm, I picked up the two empty bottles, and headed for the truck. I didn't want to stand around gawking and make a fool of myself.

"Hold on a minute," James Arness said.

I turned.

"You think about what you're doing now. You're a young man with a lot of years ahead of you. A man's got to take a little joy from his work. And if the work doesn't bring him any joy, it just might be it's time to find a new line of work."

"Thanks, Mr. Arness."

I walked back to my truck, replaced the empties in the back and climbed into the cab. I drank that ice cold Coke in three hard swigs. A long hard belch followed. It was a hot afternoon in Santa Monica. I quit that job the next day.

FREE TIME

1988

It was Friday afternoon. The bell ending the last class of the week would ring in just ten minutes. It was my second year as a teacher and I had been working at Mary McLeod Bethune Middle School for a couple of months now. Bethune was much different than my previous three teaching assignments; it was a throw away school located in South Central Los Angeles. While there were a few very good teachers at Bethune, most of the teachers were inexperienced like me or had burnt out on the profession years or even decades before. Many of the science and math classes didn't even have teachers. They were managed – no, they were mismanaged by a revolving procession of actors, writers, surfers, recent immigrants, lost souls and retirees who served as substitute teachers, most of whom understandably considered their own personal psychological and physical survival, not the education of the students, to be their chief priority. The administrators and counselors were incompetent or overwhelmed. The stench of negativity was suffocating the teaching staff, especially those of us who were new to the profession.

The principal was Lavonia "Lou" Holiday. She was a tall, slender black woman in her mid-thirties. Her nervous smile revealed a recently fitted mouthful of silver braces. While the poor woman gave it everything she had to maintain some semblance of authority, everyone knew it was Jimmy Santino, the union representative, who ran the school. He was a real character with his shoulder length, Peter Frampton hair and an endless array of flashy nylon sweat suits. Santino had a side gig coaching girl's basketball at L.A. Trade Tech and he was an uncompromising Boston Celtics fan. I came to know Jimmy Santino very well, eating lunch with him every day. He was liked by everyone, even his arch nemesis the principal. Lou Holiday never stood a chance in the battle for the hearts and minds of the teachers at Bethune. According to union regulations, Miss Holiday couldn't meet with a teacher about anything at all without Jimmy Santino in the room and most of us exercised this right. The after school meetings often included shouting matches between the first year principal and the older teachers.

"How can you talk to us about the reading levels of our students when they don't even have pencils to write with?" Mrs. Davis demanded.

"If you were dedicated to the children, you would spend a few dollars for the pencils," Lou Holiday shot back.

"If you had any dedication, you would have bought three thousand dollars worth of pencils instead of putting those silly ass braces in your middle-aged mouth!"

"Say that to me in the parking lot after the meeting, Mrs. Davis!"

Just when things were getting interesting, Jimmy Santino jumped in as peacemaker and got everybody settled down. The meetings were quite a show.

The classes were overcrowded and the students were trapped in a system that expected them to flounder in mediocrity and failure. The neighborhood was infested with gangs, a different one on every street. This was a time when irresponsible filmmakers like Dennis Hopper were giving the two largest L.A. street gangs national attention. Hopper actually awarded high profile murderers and drug dealers of the L.A. gangs with roles in his hit movie. The gang situation made me nervous at first. I can clearly remember rolling up to a stoplight on my way home from work. Dozens of rival gang members stood on opposite sides of the corner of 67th and Broadway. They were decked out in their gang colors, screaming and cursing, flashing menacing hand signs at each other. I knew enough about the neighborhood to understand these weren't just kids screwing around. Some of these guys were my age, some were considerably older. My foot rested nervously on the gas pedal, ready to accelerate as soon as the shooting started. Einstein knew what he was talking about when he said time is relative. I spent one of the longest minutes of my life waiting for that light to change. And then something very profound took place. My name rang out from the sea of red on the west side of the street.

"Hello, Mr. Snyder."

Was one of these Bloods my student? My eyes remained straight ahead; I remembered what I had learned from my water truck days, never to make eye contact with gang members, not unless they spoke to me first. Did one of them just speak to me?

"Hola, El Maestro Grande!"

A head popped out from the red mob. It was Italo Merino, a skinny little eighth grader from El Salvador. A vast carefree smile stretched across the boy's face. The kid shoved his way through the thugs, arms loaded down with books on both sides. Italo must have seen this kind of thing all the time because he didn't seem the least bit bothered or intimidated as he made his way across the street, using the crosswalk, smiling as big as day. He shoved his way through the boys in blue on the other side, nodding back to me before he disappeared into the intimidating mass. No big deal. This was Italo's neighborhood too. Maybe this new world of his wasn't any tougher than the war-torn world he had escaped down south.

The experience at 67th and Broadway rocked my world. Italo was a sweet kid, yet he survived in this place, day in and day out. I had the opportunity to return to my comfortable little house in a relatively safe neighborhood just a few miles down the Harbor Freeway each night.

Italo and the rest of my students educated me on life in a neighborhood controlled by street gangs.

"If we run out of milk, we wait 'til next day," Italo told me. "Nobody don't go out after dark. The gangsters don't like it if we go out at night. We sleep with the mattress on the floor in case somebody shooting at the house. One time the old lady next door, she die from her heart because the ambulance won't come to my street at night."

Yeah, South Central L.A. was a different world. I remember the day I was on my way to the school for the interview. Uneasiness filled me as I pulled up at a stoplight. I breathed a sigh of relief when a black and white LAPD cruiser slowed to a stop next to me. Clearly, this wasn't like the police cars I was used to seeing in the relatively peaceful neighborhoods of L.A. and its suburbs. There was no coat of wax, no Armor All on the rubber, no sparkle to the rims; this cruiser was covered with a thick coat of brown dirt. The two cops weren't like the friendly guys sporting crew cuts I was used to seeing, far from it. The driver was a tough looking black guy with long jerry curls, mysterious dark shades and a toothpick in his mouth. Sitting in the passenger seat was a massive white guy with long, greased back, blonde hair. He was wearing a dirty pair of Wayfarers with scratched up lenses, and his elbow rested on the open window. His massive, tattooed, white arm looked like it was going to explode out of his blue short sleeve. I looked over and smiled.

"How's it goin', guy?"

The white cop just turned and stared at me. For a minute there, I thought he was going to get out of the squad car and come after me. Makes a guy wonder if there might have been a couple of benign looking fellas with crew cuts in the trunk.

It seems I've gotten away from the subject at hand. When I began the story, it was a Friday afternoon like all of the others in my teaching career. I was fried. Absolutely beat. My ninth grade reading students had put in a good week. We had finished all of the activities in my lesson plans.

"Take out your independent reading books and do some reading until the end of the period."

"C'mon Mr. Snyder, be cool," Josh Howard protested.

"I thought you told me I was cool, Josh."

"Yeah, you pretty cool. But you pretty stressed out too."

"So?"

"So it's Friday and we all need a break. You need a break too, Mr. Snyder. Why don't you give us some free time?"

"Free time?"

I knew free time was a buzzword and it could mean real trouble. At least that's what my district appointed teaching advisor had told me. She said that I should always provide the students with more work than they could possibly finish, that free time could lead to chaos. I didn't want chaos. Nobody wants chaos. On the other hand, I had never actually met my teaching advisor. She taught at a school in an affluent neighborhood on the other side of the Hollywood Hills. I'd only spoken with her on the phone a couple of times. What could she possibly know about Josh, Italo, and the rest of the kids in South Central? How was I supposed to know if she did know what she was talking about?

"C'mon, Mr. Snyder, be cool. We tired."

Josh flashed his magnificent, winning smile. The rest of the students got behind him. They were all asking for free time.

"Why not?" I relented. "We all deserve a break, don't we? Everybody go ahead and relax."

The bargaining process had taken up a couple of minutes. The bell was going to ring in seven minutes. How much chaos could possibly manifest in seven minutes? Leaning back in my swivel chair, I placed my hands behind my head. I was damned tired. I took a deep breath.

CRASH!

It was the sound of a desk flying across the room and shattering against the chalkboard.

"What you call me, you bitch?"

It was Florence and Leticia standing nose to nose. They were both breathing fire.

"I called you a ho! And you a nasty ass bitch, too!"

Just like that, it was on. Leticia threw the first punch, a perfect right cross solidly connected to the side of Florence's head. Florence came back with a couple of crisp left jabs to her opponent's face. And then they let loose on each other, both girls throwing and landing fast, hard head shots. Never in my life had I seen girls fight with such style, aggression, and accuracy.

This all took place in less than five seconds. Once everything registered, I reacted, lumbering across the room, coming up behind the belligerent girls and scooping them up by their necks, each of them in a firm headlock under both of my arms.

"Alright girls, that's enough," I said. It was the most teacheresque line I could come up with. I dragged them toward the hallway.

Leticia began to pull hard against my headlock.

"Take it easy L…"

I was going to say Leticia. My tongue was in place between my teeth to say Leticia. That's when Leticia delivered a perfectly executed uppercut to the bottom of my chin. Leticia's fist drove my bottom teeth up into my top teeth, splitting open my tongue which was lodged between. It hurt like hell. Not that I was ever any kind of street fighter, but I've been tagged a few times and I'm telling you right now, this was the hardest I've ever been hit. Blood shot from my tongue and poured out of my mouth and onto my white shirt. Aftershocks from the blow were reverberating through my skull. To this day, I am mystified when I try to figure out how Leticia got the upper cut off while in a headlock.

"How you like that, bitch?" Leticia asked triumphantly.

"You hit me, Leticia," I said.

"Oh I'm sorry, Mr. Snyder, but I'm gonna kill that bitch!" Leticia shouted as she struggled to wriggle herself loose from my lock.

"Oooh! Mr. Snyder got socked!" somebody shouted.

Clamping down hard on Leticia's neck, I picked up the pace. I wasn't interested in taking any more shots. My pulse throbbed away in my rapidly inflating tongue. Lukewarm blood was teeming off of my chin and onto my neck and shirt. The bell rang. Students exploded into the hallways.

"Look at Mr. Snyder!" someone shouted. "He has blood squirting from his face!"

"It's quite obviously the result of a ruptured artery," some brainy looking substitute science teacher popped off.

Mitch Yount, the surfer teacher from across the hall, approached.

"Let me help you out buddy. Girl fight, huh?"

"Thath white," I tried to answer.

My tongue had swelled measurably by now.

"You got some serious fountain action goin' there, Snyder. Looks like someone connected with an artery."

He was absolutely right. In my peripheral vision, I could see a thin red stream squirting hard from my tongue like a leak in a garden hose. It looked downright surreal. I mean, it's not every day you see a stream of blood spouting from your own mouth.

"Let me take Leticia," Yount said

"Wath out, theeth guwth know how to thwow a uppa cuth."

I was trying to say, "Watch out, these girls know how to throw an uppercut."

Miraculously, he understood.

"I'd say one of 'em sure as hell does," Mitch said with a smile.

Just then, school security showed up to take the girls off our hands.

"Come down to the office when you get cleaned up. You really need to call for help when you get into this kind of trouble, Mr. Snyder," the security guard with dreadlocks said. He shook his head from side to side and gave me his most condescending look.

Josh Howard handed me a wet paper towel.

"Here you go, Mr. Snyder."

"Thankth, Dwoth."

I tried to say *Thanks Josh* as I plugged up my leak with the towel. I could feel the swelling getting worse.

"Does that hurt, Mr. Snyder?"

Josh was intently staring at me with his head tilted to one side.

"Of coth it huth, Yoth."

"That's weird, Mr. Snyder. I didn't know blood could do that," Josh said.

"Just a small artery rupture, Josh," Yount said. He turned to me, "You just never know when you're gonna find teachable moments like this, Mr. Snyder. So it was Leticia that popped you?"

"Thath wythe, thee goth be bith a ubbu cuth."

It was impossible to say anything that remotely sounded like *she got me with an upper cut* now that my tongue had swelled to the size of a submarine sandwich.

"Got to remember to protect yourself at all times, Snyder," Yount said, fighting back laughter.

I guessed Mitch Yount would a have a good story to tell his surfing buddies at the Manhattan Beach pier Saturday morning. Yount was okay with me. I would have probably laughed too if the shoe had been on the other foot. I might have laughed right then and there if my tongue hadn't been so freakishly swollen.

My meals would be taken through a straw for the next few days.

More than eighteen years have passed since that gruesome tongue-splitting afternoon. Whenever a student asks me to allot free time in the classroom, I tell them about Leticia's uppercut, the ruptured tongue artery, and taking meals through a straw. I don't think they believe me and I know they think I'm a little strange, but it never fails to put an end to the subject of free time.

I hate free time.

That's all, folks.

Photo: Clifton Batchelor

William Snyder was born in 1960 in Hawthorne, California. For twenty-five years he has taught in California and Arizona schools. He has also performed as a stand-up comedian and written and hosted educational television programming. He lives with his wife and daughters in Arizona.

Made in the USA
Charleston, SC
18 February 2013